D1360546

CLASSIC SERMONS

ON THE

RESURRECTION OF CHRIST

CLASSIC SERMONS Series

Classic Sermons on the Attributes of God
Classic Sermons on the Birth of Christ
Classic Sermons on Christian Service
Classic Sermons on the Cross of Christ
Classic Sermons on Faith and Doubt
Classic Sermons on Family and Home
Classic Sermons on Heaven and Hell
Classic Sermons on Hope
Classic Sermons on the Names of God
Classic Sermons on Overcoming Fear
Classic Sermons on Prayer
Classic Sermons on Praise
Classic Sermons on the Prodigal Son
Classic Sermons on the Resurrection of Christ
Classic Sermons on the Second Coming and
　　Other Prophetic Themes
Classic Sermons on the Sovereignty of God
Classic Sermons on Spiritual Warfare
Classic Sermons on Suffering
Classic Sermons on Worship

CLASSIC SERMONS

ON THE

RESURRECTION

OF CHRIST

Compiled by
Warren W. Wiersbe

HENDRICKSON PUBLISHERS

Classic Sermons on the Resurrection of Christ
Hendrickson Publishers, Inc. edition
ISBN 1-56563-071-8

This edition is published by special arrangement with
and permission of Kregel Publications. Copyright © 1991
by Kregel Publications, a division of Kregel, Inc. P.O. Box
2607, Grand Rapids, MI 49501.

Printed in the United States of America

CONTENTS

5

PREFACE

THE *KREGEL CLASSIC SERMONS SERIES* is an attempt to assemble and publish meaningful sermons from master preachers about significant themes.

These are *sermons*, not essays or chapters taken from books about themes. Not all of these sermons could be called "great," but all of them are *meaningful*. They apply the truths of the Bible to the needs of the human heart, which is something that all effective preaching must do.

While some are better known than others, all of the preachers, whose sermons I have selected, had important ministries and were highly respected in their day. The fact that a sermon is included in this volume does not mean that either the compiler or the publisher agrees with or endorses everything that the man did, preached, or wrote. The sermon is here because it has a valued contribution to make.

These are sermons about *significant* themes. The pulpit is no place to play with trivia. The preacher has thirty minutes in which to help mend broken hearts, change defeated lives, and save lost souls; and he can never accomplish this demanding ministry by distributing homiletical tidbits. In these difficult days, we do not need "clever" pulpiteers who discuss the times; we need dedicated ambassadors who will preach the eternities.

The reading of these sermons can enrich your own spiritual life. The studying of them can enrich your own skills as an interpreter and expounder of God's truth. However God uses these sermons in your own life and ministry, my prayer is that His Church around the world will be encouraged and strengthened.

WARREN W. WIERSBE

"Christ Is Risen! He Is Risen Indeed!"

Walter A. Maier (1893-1950) was known around the world as the speaker on "The Lutheran Hour," heard over more than a thousand radio stations. Many of his faithful listeners did not realize that this effective communicator was also professor of Old Testament and Semitic Languages at Concordia Seminary in St. Louis. It was said that Maier spent one hour in preparation for each minute that he spoke on the radio. Many of his radio sermons were published in volumes still treasured by those who appreciate good preaching.

This sermon is found in *Peace Through Christ*, published by Concordia Publishing House, St. Louis, in 1940.

Walter A. Maier

1

"CHRIST IS RISEN!
HE IS RISEN INDEED!"

As Christ was raised up from the dead by the glory of the
Father, even so we also should walk in newness of life
(Romans 6:4).

THE UNITED STATES is one of the few countries in which
the customary Easter-greetings contain no reference to
the resurrection of Jesus Christ. Throughout the Greek-
speaking world, for example, Christians address one
another in the same Easter salutation that rang through
the early church, *"Christos anestee!"* "Christ is risen!" and
with the ancient response, *"Aleethoos anestee,"* "He is
truly risen!" In the Latin church of the first centuries the
Easter-greeting was, *"Vivit!"* "He lives!" and the reply, *"Vere
Vivit!"* "He lives indeed!" In Spanish lands Christians say
"Cristo vive!" In Germany believers, no matter to which
church they may belong, salute one another with exultant
joy: *"Der Herr ist auferstanden!"* and the reply, *"Er ist
wahrhaftig auferstanden!"* Even in Russia, where
Communist slogans have not altogether banished the
reverence for God's truth, loyal followers of Christ, meeting
their kindred in the faith, say, *"Christos Voskres!"* and
receive the reply, *"Voistinu Voskres!"* All these expressions
serve one thought and purpose: they glorify the risen
Savior.

In our country, however, we say, "Happy Easter!"
forgetting that the word "Easter" may have no connection
with the open grave and in no way testifies to the
resurrection miracle. Because the Savior's triumph over
the tomb, together with the crucifixion, which preceded it,
are the most blessed of all truths, and Christians should
follow the angel's command, *"Go quickly and tell His
disciples!"* instead of limiting their Easter conversation to

9

the subjects of new clothes, spring hats, festive food, holiday programs, post-Lenten parties, we ask you who are the Lord's to help inaugurate and maintain a Christ-exalting movement by which believers in all churches greet one another on this day with the salutation, "Christ is risen!" and respond, "He is risen indeed!"

On the first Easter only a few followers of the Savior could sound that triumphant note; but on this 1940 Easter, when over the 171 stations in our "Bringing-Christ-to-the-Nation" broadcasting system millions can hear the message of our Lord's victory over death, multitudes should heed the plea to keep Jesus in Easter by greeting every one whom they meet before the close of this day with the faith-born declaration, "Christ is risen!" May God give every one of you the resolution to proclaim, "He is risen indeed!"

To strengthen our faith in the resurrection reality, let us—and I include especially the doubtful and uncertain, even the scoffers and atheists in this audience—stand once more in spirit before the rock-hewn grave in Joseph's garden, where the broken seal, the removed stone, the prostrate Roman guard, the empty tomb, the discarded burial shroud, the white-robed angel with his announcement, "He *is not here but is risen!*" (Matt. 28:6) all combine to impress us with the holy, heavenly truth that Jesus, God's Son and the world's Savior, has eternally defeated death for Himself and for all men. With the Easter cry,

"Christ Is Risen! He Is Risen Indeed!"

we invite you, rather, we urgently plead with you, to study and believe the inspired resurrection message of Saint Paul (Romans 6:4), "*As Christ was raised up from the dead by the glory of the Father, even so we also should walk in newness of life,*" and by the Spirit's guidance to find the Easter truth and the Easter newness.

The Easter Truth

When the apostle summarizes the triumph of this sacred day in the seven short words "*Christ was raised up from the dead!"* he regards the mysterious but magnificent bursting of the grave as an unquestionable, supreme truth. In the entire New Testament record the resurrection victory is never debated; no lengthy defenses of its facts are offered; no attempts are made to vindicate the details in the Easter narratives. Throughout the Scriptures and the early church the declaration that "on the third day He rose again from the dead" is uncompromisingly accepted as the great climax truth of our faith, the necessary keystone in the arch of our hope. No resurrection, no redemption! No open grave, no opened heaven! No risen Christ, no risen Christians! This is the unavoidable alternative: *"If Christ be not risen, then is our preaching vain. . . . Yea, and we are found false witnesses of God. . . . If Christ be not raised, your faith is vain; ye are yet in your sins. Then they also which are fallen asleep in Christ are perished"* (1 Cor. 15:14-18). Yet, as Paul triumphed, *"Now is Christ risen,"* so I want your faith to ring, clear and unhesitating. Some of you doubt or deny the angelic proclamation, *"He is risen!"* because you have never taken the time to behold the Easter evangel with open eyes. You have had your mind poisoned by a destructive teacher, an atheist agitator or an applauded skeptic. Will you not be fair enough to read through the New Testament evidence for the Savior's restoration to life?

If you submit to the Spirit's guidance, you will experience the same startling reverse that challenged the life of Gilbert West. He thought that he had found confusion and contradiction in the four gospel accounts, and his exposure, he boasted, would reveal the complete impossibility of the open grave. When he had finished his investigations, however, he penned this remarkable confession: "As I have studied the evidence for the resurrection of Jesus Christ from the dead and have weighed it according to the laws of evidence, I have become satisfied that Jesus really rose from the dead, as recorded in the gospels, and I have written my book" (the book that was to destroy all faith in the Resurrection) "on that side"— the side of Christ and His truth.

More recently we have witnessed a similar challenging

change from wavering doubt to convicted faith. Frank Morison, acclaimed for his recent book on Pontius Pilate, tells us that, when as a young man he began seriously to study Christ's life, he had the definite feeling that the New Testament Scriptures rested on very insecure foundation. Higher critics and professional enemies of the Bible had given him the impression that God's Word was unreliable. The few things that these destructionists left standing the physical science courses in which he was enrolled proceeded to undermine. Scientific thought was obstinately opposed to every miracle. He had read the great Huxley's verdict, "Miracles do not happen!" and had come to the conclusion that the laws of the universe could never be suspended. He could not, however, entirely subdue a reverent regard for our Lord acquired during his childhood; and in order to find peace of mind, he decided to study the Savior's suffering and resurrection. He proposed to strip the Scriptural record "of its overgrowth of primitive beliefs and dogmatic suppositions." He would see Jesus as He really was, not as the Christians believed Him to be. Hardly, however, had he plunged into the eternal Word, when his thoughts concerning Christ were revolutionized. What he calls "the irresistible logic" of the gospel narrative gripped his heart; he found that he could not write a book attacking the Savior's death and resurrection; instead, he published a volume on the first Easter, a reverent defense of Bible truth.

You, too, will be able to overcome doubt and to exult with the apostle, *"Christ was raised up from the dead,"* if you prayerfully approach the Easter-story, asking for the Spirit's strength and light as you study its statements. The trouble with most people who reject the Easter gospel is not to be found in any insurmountable opposition by their brain processes, but in their stubborn unwillingness to concede the truth. A brilliant New York attorney is quoted as admitting, "I am convinced that Jesus really did rise from the dead, but I am no nearer to being a Christian than I was before. I thought that the difficulty was with my head. I find that it really is with my heart."

Evidences of Christ's Resurrection

How convincing, however, the Easter evidence is when both the head and the heart accept Christ! Thomas Arnold, beloved headmaster at Rugby, asserted that no fact of history is so well attested as the Savior's resurrection; and assuredly an imposing array of witnesses declares its complete, eternal verity! Listen to their testimony!

Mary Magdalene, who hastened to the tomb even before daybreak, the first in all the world to meet the resurrected Savior, asserted, *"I have seen the Lord!"* The other women who lingered long at the cross on Good Friday and who likewise came early on that Sunday morning to embalm the Savior's body, found the stone rolled away and an angel of the Lord, clothed with raiment white as dazzling snow. *"He is not here, He is risen,"* was the cry that greeted them. They could explain how as they left the empty tomb they met Jesus, heard Him speak joy to their hearts, fell at His feet and worshiped Him. Simon Peter, restored by a glance of his Savior's grace, knelt before his resurrected Lord, and though the Scriptures give us no details of the meeting, we may well believe Peter could testify that Jesus raised nail-scarred hands in benediction on him who was to become the rock disciple. James, one of our Lord's brethren, who at first did not accept Him as God's Son and the world's Savior, likewise stood face to face with Jesus; and if he could give his testimony to our radio audience, he would assert that his whole life was rebuilt and purified through this contact. Thomas, the doubting, who would not believe unless he saw the print of the nails and put his own fingers into those scars, mounts the witness stand in behalf of Jesus to announce that he did behold the wounded hands and feet, the riven side, and that we shall be blessed if we believe even though we do not see. The two disciples on the Emmaus road who were filled with unspeakable joy when Christ *"went in to tarry with them;"* the entire company of disciples, who had hid themselves behind shut doors and suddenly saw that the glorified Savior was in their midst to declare, *"Peace be unto you!"*; the seven followers who went fishing with the resurrected Christ and with Him ate breakfast on the shore; the five hundred believers who in one manifestation beheld the Lord, perhaps on Mount Tabor in Galilee; and the Eleven who were with Christ on Mount Olivet at His ascension—all these, together with the mighty missionary Saint Paul, who actually saw his glorified Savior on the Damascus road and then went out to start the conquest of the world for Him, are personal, competent witnesses to this miracle of the ages. If their testimony, combined and detailed as it is, does not convince the most skeptical of Christ's resurrection, the difficulty lies not in the Easter truth but in the refusal to bow before that truth.

So convincing is the evidence that, when submitted to careful scrutiny by legal experts, it has been thoroughly vindicated. In a remarkable book by Simon Greenleaf a special section is devoted to the Resurrection, with the result that the Gospel narratives are completely endorsed. Some of you say, however, "Who is this Simon Greenleaf? Is his opinion recognized?" Let me answer not only that he was professor of law at Harvard and perhaps the most distinguished jurist ever connected with that eminent university, but also that the *London Law Magazine* called him one of the most highly esteemed legal authorities of his century, asserting that he has shed more light on the laws of evidence than all lawyers who adorn the courts of Europe. Now, if that distinguished authority unreservedly endorses the resurrection, why does any one in this audience hesitate to subscribe to its complete truth?

Every Sunday, the day of worship selected by the early church because Christ rose on Sunday; every baptism, the sacred Christian rite instituted by the risen Christ; every church and mission preaching the glorious message that Jesus has conquered death for all men—these are the incontestable proofs of the Easter fact, proofs, however, which those who are Christ's do not need, since they have the Spirit's testimony in their hearts.

You see, Jesus had to rise from the grave. It was clearly foretold in the Old Testament and plainly predicted by the Savior Himself; and before God's holy Word can be broken,—remember this, my discouraged friends who need a firm foundation for your hope,—everything on, under, and over this world will collapse into dust. The Scriptures cannot fail; and God's guaranty for the Bible's every promise of comfort and sustaining love is to be found at the open grave. "Christ is risen! He is risen indeed!"

The Resurrection Proves That Christ Has Power Over Life and Death

Jesus had to be resurrected from the dead to prove that He is no mere mortal leader of human theorist but God Almighty, with power over life and death. During recent weeks worldwide attention has been focused on a remarkable discovery in Egypt. After years of plodding search scientists uncovered a secret, concealed tomb. When the debris of centuries was removed and the door, solemnly sealed 3,000 years ago, was opened with appropriate ceremonies, there, in an imposing burial chamber, amid gold ornaments and almost priceless jewels, lay a mysterious mummy case of granite. Beneath it was a second sarcophagus of silver and below that another covering of solid gold. Within lay the remains of Pharaoh Psou-Sennes. A thousand years before Christ he ruled Upper and Lower Egypt with an iron hand. Princes, priests, and people bowed abjectly before him, but finally he bowed before death. Despite his money and men he could not escape from the tomb; and within that mummy case, which will soon be a museum exhibit, his shriveled, blackened corpse testifies to the relentless grip of the grave. How our hallelujahs should ring out today when the open grave testifies that Jesus Christ was very God of very God, the Ruler of life and of death itself! "The Lord is risen! He is risen indeed!"

No other explanation for the open tomb has ever been able to satisfy the human mind. Unbelievers used to say that Jesus had merely swooned when taken from the cross; only apparently dead, He was later revived in the grave. But the Roman soldiers knew better; they were so positive that He had breathed His last that they did not follow the usual custom of breaking His legs. Skeptics used to assert, repeating a first-century falsehood, that the Roman guards slept at their posts and Christ's disciples, under the cover of darkness, stole His body. Yet even the bribery of the priests could not make this story plausible. It meant death for a Roman soldier to fall asleep on duty. Besides, it would tax any one's imagination to believe that the great stone could be rolled away, the official seal broken, and a company of men go in and out the grave to remove a corpse without being heard or seen. Infidels used to claim that the Resurrection rests on the fantasy of hallucinated women and suggestible followers; but even open critics have rejected this absurd theory. Thus you can bring one attempt after the other to take the supernatural out of the Easter miracle and to account for it on purely human premises, but each endeavor is doomed to abject failure. Only one explanation remains: Christ rose from the dead because He was the all-powerful God, with the divine omnipotence required to destroy death! "Christ is risen! He is risen indeed!"

The Resurrection Was the Crowning Climax of God's Love

Christ had to rise from the dead because His resurrection was the crowning climax of His love. Had He stayed in the grave, not only would His promises of new life have been unfulfilled and His claims for divine power disproved, but His entire suffering, the agony of the cross, the God-forsakenness, and the never-to-be-fathomed sorrow that crushed His soul, would have been in vain. The entire purpose of His incarnation would have remained unaccomplished. When, however, on that bright Easter morning, the power of earth and hell, the priestly craftiness, and the official guard, the rock-hewn grave and the impressive seal at its entrance, the winding linen and the burial shrouds, could not keep Jesus in the tomb, it was Heaven's highest proof that Calvary's one sacrifice for the sins of all ages had been accepted, that Jesus' blood had not been shed in vain, that as Christ *"was delivered for our offences,"* so He *"was raised again for our justification"* (Rom. 4:25).

This trust is indicated in our text when it declares

"Christ was raised up from the dead by *the Glory of the Father.*" Easter is Heaven's glorious seal, God's glorious endorsement, the Father's glorious acceptance of His Son's self-sacrifice for the world's sins. Easter is the promise of peace and pardon to every one who believes. Therefore, in the name of the risen Christ, I ask you, whoever you are, do you subscribe to the seven simple words of our text, *"Christ was raised up from the dead"*? It matters little what your opinion may be on a thousand other issues, past, present, and future; but for the sake of your soul, believe the resurrection miracle! Stifle gain-saying doubts that demand, "How could Christ return to life?" Turn away from skeptical, sneering men of affairs to the resolute faith of the mighty leaders in science, culture, and progress who have joyfully accepted the Easter miracle! Today with unquestioning trust take God at His word! Ask Him for strength to overcome every uncertainty, and if you follow the promptings of the Spirit that now asks you to acclaim Christ, you, too, will be led, as doubting Thomas was, to behold the Savior with a confidence that says, "My Lord, my God, my ever-living Savior!" You, too, will gladly tell all whom you meet, "Christ is risen! He is risen indeed!"

The Resurrection Brings Newness of Life and Hope

Without this radiant joy, life must lose its beauty and blessing. Herbert Spencer, England's learned philosopher, did not accept the Easter victory; yet in his last hours he asked that only one word be chiseled on his tombstone, the Latin *Infelicissimus,* meaning "The most unhappy one." The rejection of the Easter victory always leaves men without hope, while humble confidence in this truth bestows new assurance.

It is this newness for which our text appeals when it says, "As Christ was raised from the dead, . . . *even so we also should walk in newness of life.*" When Jesus rose from the tomb, an entirely new era dawned on the world; a New Testament was offered to men in which the most persistent and overpowering terror, the cringing before the grave, was removed for all who acclaim Jesus their Savior. What trembling the thoughts of death often provoke! Classify the fears and phobias of men in any way you will; add up the fright caused by sickness, age, loss, imprisonment, dishonor, and the sum total will be far below the heart-sinking surrender to despair, which often marks life's end.

Ask a soldier who has seen godless scoffers go over the top and face death in No Man's Land how they chatter and quake; ask a sailor who has stood with infidels in ghastly consternation; ask a doctor to describe the last moments of blasphemers, when the terrors of hell are written on their faces as shuddering curses leap from their lips, and you will understand that the most crushing of earth's other burdens is not to be compared with what men often fear in their last moments. We hear of exceptions, it is true; a disillusionized woman writing "Exit smiling!" on the walls of her hotel room and then plunging from her high window to a splattering death on the sidewalk below; a convicted murderer approaching the gallows with swaggering unconcern; highly emotional sufferers wishing themselves dead. But unless the conscience is altogether destroyed, every one who is without Christ shrinks from death. Men know, although they may glibly deny the existence of God and ridicule the mention of heaven and hell, that there is a judgment, a retribution, a punishment beyond the grave. We need not argue this fact with any one in our audience; the solemn warning voice tells you that you cannot live in sin and hope to escape punishment. But I do need to show many what Christ and the Easter resurrection can mean to them; for ignorance and superstition concerning the future existence are blighting the lives of millions. If the census enumerators, whose activities have been widely discussed in our newspapers, should ask the 130,000,000 Americans to express their hopes for the hereafter, the answers would be bewildering and contradictory; but on Easter, if we ask Christ concerning eternity, He points us both to the open grave and the open heaven to say: *"Because I live, ye shall live also!" "I am the resurrection and the life: he that believeth in Me, though he were dead, yet shall he live!" "In My Father's house are many mansions: . . . I go to prepare a place for you"* (John 14:19; 11:25; 14:2).

The Resurrection Guarantees Your Resurrection

As you read these and scores of other passages promising a blessed eternity with Jesus, thank God that no hesitation or uncertainty lingers behind His pledges. They are the highest truths that even Heaven knows. With the Easter faith in your heart, you need not grovel in despair to ask, "What will become of me when life stops?" You, the mortally sick, the invalids whose existence hangs on a thin, shortened thread; you in the prime and strength of life who may be cut down by the sudden accidents that lurk closely and loom frequently on the pathways of our modern life—believe that Christ's resurrection guarantees your resurrection! Easter is the divine warrant that God has forgiven the sins which bring eternal death as their wages. This holy day offers the surety that God has accepted the suffering and dying of His own Son as the payment for your sins and the ransom for their punishment. Knowing that your transgressions are nailed to the cross and that Christ is the living, divine Savior and not a dead deceiver, you can confidently believe that the grave does not end all; that you can escape the terrors of hell and be blessed in heaven, before the presence of Jesus. For here is that plain but powerful promise of life, *"God so loved the world that He gave His only begotten Son, that whosoever believeth in Him should not perish, but have everlasting life"* (John 3:16).

It is true that temporal death comes to every one of us, as it came to Christ; but it is only a passing instantaneous change from our earthly existence to that incomparably more blessed heavenly life. For at the open grave we learn through faith that we are more than creatures of accident, controlled by a cold, cruel fate, directed toward everlasting discard and decay; rather, that we are God's children of holy destiny, who come from God and, through His Son, will return to Him.

With the fear of death removed—and how confidently Christians can long for eternity!—with heavenly bliss positively promised all believers, you can understand why our text beseeches us *"to walk in newness of life."* Easter tells us that old fears, old weaknesses, old sorrows, old doubts, are all passed away in the newness of the Savior's resurrection. Does anything keep you from this blessed newness? Do old, heavy problems lurk in your soul beneath new Easter garments? Analyze them in this day's radiance, and their darkness will disappear. Are your troubles money difficulties, family quarrels, questions of health? Are you the victim of malicious plotting, crooked politics, and hateful revenge? Stand before the empty tomb to realize that the Christ who has the power over death can control these smaller issues in your life and turn your crosses to advantages, as the Good Friday defeat gave way to the Easter victory. Whatever your personal problems may be, the tragedy that your husband has lost his God and his love for you; the cutting blow that after years of faithful, unselfish service you have been cast aside; especially the recurrence of private sins, repeated concessions to wrong, worry over your salvation and spiritual condition—look to the heavens reopened by the resurrection and know that *the sufferings of this present time are not worthy to be compared with the glory which shall be revealed in us"* (Rom. 8:18)! Trust Christ implicitly! Trust Him even though it seems that He permits you to be crushed under the weight of affliction! For finally, in God's good time and in His blessed way, the dawn of deliverance will break, and the new day will find you stronger because of your night of anguish.

Has the deepest sorrow, bereavement, darkened your home? Does it seem to you that the last glimmering joy of your life has disappeared with the death of a beloved one? Instead of questioning the Father's love and goodness in allowing your husband, the mainstay of your home, or an only child, the center of your affections, to be snatched away by death, dry your tears, strengthen your heart through Christ, and remember that Easter proves that God's way with His children is always the road to redemption and victory! Behold Jesus emerging from the tomb and take heart in the Easter comfort that all God's beloved, through Christ, will come forth to life eternal!

Commit yourselves wholly to the risen Christ on Easter, the day especially appropriate for dedication to the Savior!

Take your sins and weaknesses, lay them at the foot of the cross, hasten to the open grave, and there you will find newness of life, forgiveness of your transgressions, a fortifying of your faith, and the joy of assured salvation! For Easter, blessed Easter, is yours for life and death, with this triumph of trust: "Christ is risen! He is risen indeed!"

The Grave of the Dead John and the Grave of the Living Jesus

Alexander Maclaren (1826-1910) was one of Great Britain's most famous preachers. While pastoring the Union Chapel, Manchester (1858-1903), he became known as "the prince of expository preachers." Rarely active in denominational or civic affairs, Maclaren invested his time studying the Word in the original and sharing its truths with others in sermons that are still models of effective expository preaching. He published a number of books of sermons and climaxed his ministry by publishing his monumental *Expositions of Holy Scripture*.

This message is taken from *The Secret of Power* (Funk & Wagnalls, New York, 1902).

Alexander Maclaren

2

THE GRAVE OF THE DEAD JOHN AND THE GRAVE OF THE LIVING JESUS

And John's disciples came, and took up the body, and buried it, and went and told Jesus (Matthew 14:12).

And they departed quickly from the sepulcher with fear and great joy (Matthew 28:8).

THERE IS A remarkable parallel and still more remarkable contrast between these two groups of disciples at the graves of their respective masters. John the Baptist's followers venture into the very jaws of the lion to rescue the headless corpse of their martyred teacher from a prison grave. They bear it away and lay it reverently in its unknown sepulcher, and when they have done these last offices of love they feel that all is over. They have no longer a center, and they disintegrate. There was nothing to hold them together any more. The shepherd had been smitten, and the flock were scattered. As a "school" or a distinct community they cease to be, and are mostly absorbed into the ranks of Christ's followers. That sorrowful little company that turned from John's grave, perhaps amidst the grim rocks of Moab, perhaps in his native city amongst the hills of Judah, parted, then, to meet no more, and to bear away only a common sorrow that time would comfort, and a common memory that time would dim.

The other group laid their martyred Master in His grave with as tender hands and as little hope as did John's disciples. The bond that held them together was gone too, and the disintegrating process began at once. We see them breaking up into little knots, and soon they, too, will be scattered. The women come to the grave to perform the woman's office of anointing, and they are left to go alone. Other slight hints are given which show how much the ties of companionship had been relaxed, even in a day, and how certainly and quickly they would have fallen asunder. But all at once a new element comes in, all is changed. The earliest visitors to the sepulcher leave it, not with the lingering sorrow of those who have no more that they can do, but with the quick buoyant step of people charged with great and glad tidings. They come to it wrapped in grief—they leave it with great joy. They come to it, feeling that all was over, and their union with the rest who had loved Him was little more than a remembrance. They go away feeling that they are bound together more closely than ever.

The grave of John was the end of a "school." The grave of Jesus was the beginning of the church. Why? The only answer is the message which the women brought back from the empty sepulcher on that Easter day: "The Lord is risen." The whole history of the Christian church, and even its very existence, is unintelligible, except on the supposition of the resurrection. But for that, the fate of John's disciples would have been the fate of Christ's— they would have melted away into the mass of the nation, and at most there would have been one more petty Galilean sect, that would have lived on for a generation and died out when the last of His companions died.

So from these two contrasted groups we may fairly gather some thoughts as to the resurrection of Christ, as attested by the very existence of a Christian church, and as to the joy of that resurrection.

The Resurrection United the Disciples

Now the first point to be considered is that the conduct of Christ's disciples after His death was exactly the opposite of what might have been expected.

They held together. The natural thing for them to do would have been to disband; for the one bond was gone; and if they had acted according to the ordinary laws of human conduct they would have said to themselves, Let us go back to our fishing-boats and our tax-gathering, and seek safety in separation, and nurse our sorrow apart. A few lingering days might have been given to weep together at His grave, and to assuage the first bitterness of grief and disappointment; but when these were over, nothing could have prevented Christianity and the church from being buried in the same sepulcher as Jesus. As certainly as the stopping up of the fountain would empty the river's bed, so surely would Christ's death have scattered His disciples. And that strange fact, that it did not scatter them, needs to be looked well into and fairly accounted for in some plausible manner. The end of John's school gives a parallel which brings the singularity of the fact into the stronger relief; and looking at these two groups as they stand before us in these two texts, the question is irresistibly suggested, Why did not the one fall away into its separate elements, as the other did? The keystone of the arch was in both cases withdrawn—why did the one structure topple into ruin while the other stood firm?

Not only did the disciples of Christ keep united, but their conceptions of Jesus underwent a remarkable change, on His death. We might have expected indeed that, when memory began to work, and the disturbing influence of daily association was withdrawn, the same idealizing process would have begun on their image of Him, which reveals and ennobles the characters of our dear ones who have gone away from us. Most men have to die before their true beauty is discerned. But no process of that sort will suffice to account for the change and heightening of the disciples' thoughts about their dead Lord. It was not merely that, as they remembered, they said, Did not our hearts burn within us by the way while He talked with us?—but that His death wrought exactly the opposite effect from what it might have been expected to do. It ought to have ended their hope that He was the Messiah, and we know that within forty-eight hours it was beginning to do so, as we learn from the plaintive words of disappointed and fading hope: "We trusted that it had been He which should have redeemed Israel." If, so early, the cold conviction was stealing over their hearts that their dearest expectation was proved by His death to have been a dream, what could have prevented its entire dominion over them, as the days grew into months and years? But somehow or other that process was arrested, and the opposite one set in. The death that should have shattered Messianic dreams confirmed them. The death that should have cast a deeper shadow of incomprehensibleness over His strange and lofty claims poured a new light upon them, which made them all plain and clear. The very pats of His teaching which His death would have made those who loved Him wish to forget, became the center of His followers' faith. His cross became His throne. While He lived with them they knew not what He said in His deepest words, but, by a strange paradox, His death convinced them that He was the Son of God, and that that which they had seen with their eyes, and their hands had handled, was the eternal life. The cross alone could never have done that. Something else there must have been, if the men were sane, to account for this paradox.

Nor is this all. Another equally unlikely sequel of the death of Jesus is the unmistakable moral transformation effected on the disciples. Timorous and tremulous before, something or other touched them into altogether new boldness and self-possession. Dependent on His presence before, and helpless when He was away from them for an hour, they become all at once strong and calm; they stand before the fury of a Jewish mob and the threatenings of the Sanhedrin, unmoved and victorious. And these brave confessors and saintly heroes are the men who, a few weeks before, had been petulant, self-willed, jealous, cowardly. What had lifted them suddenly so far above themselves? Their Master's death? That would more naturally have taken any heart of courage out of them, and left them indeed as sheep in the midst of wolves. Why, then, do they thus strangely blaze up into grandeur and heroism? Can any reasonable account be given of these paradoxes? Surely it is not too much to ask of people who profess to explain Christianity on naturalistic principles, that they shall make the process clear to us by which, Christ being dead and buried, His disciples were kept together, learned to think more loftily of Him and sprang at once to a new grandeur of character. Why did they not do as John's disciples did, and disappear? Why was not the stream lost in the sand, when the head-waters were cut off?

The Resurrection Attested by the Church

Notice then, next, that the disciples' immediate belief in the Resurrection furnishes a reasonable, and the only reasonable, explanation of the facts. There is no better historical evidence of a fact than the existence of an institution built upon it, and coeval with it. The Christian church is such evidence for the fact of the Resurrection; or, to put the conclusion in the most moderate fashion, for the belief in the Resurrection. For, as we have shown, the natural effect of our Lord's death would have been to shatter the whole fabric: and if that effect were not produced, the only reasonable account of the force that hindered it is, that His followers believed that He rose again. Since that was their faith, one can understand how they were banded more closely together than ever. One can understand how their eyes were opened to know Him who was "declared to be the Son of God with power by the resurrection from the dead." One can understand how, in the enthusiasm of these new thoughts of their Lord, and in the strength of His victory over death, they put aside their old fears and littlenesses and clothed themselves in armor of light. "The Lord is risen indeed" was the belief which made the continuous existence of the church possible. Any other explanation of that great outstanding fact is lame and hopelessly insufficient.

We know that that belief was the belief of the early church. Even if one waived all reference to the gospels we have the means of demonstrating that in Paul's undisputed epistles. Nobody has questioned that he wrote the First Epistle to the Corinthians. The date most generally assumed to that letter brings it within about twenty-five years of the crucifixion. In that letter, in addition to a multitude of incidental references to the Lord as risen, we have the great passage in the fifteenth chapter, where the apostle not only declares that the Resurrection was one of the two facts which made his "gospel," but solemnly enumerates the witnesses of the risen Lord, and alleges that this gospel of the resurrection was common to him and to all the church. He tells us of Christ's appearance to himself at his conversion, which must have taken place within six or seven years of the crucifixion, and assures us that at that early period he found the whole church believing and preaching Christ's resurrection. Their belief rested on their alleged meeting with Him a few days after his death, and it is inconceivable that within so short a period such a belief should have sprung up and been universally received if it had not begun when and as they said it did.

But we are not left even to inferences of this kind to show that from the beginning the church witnessed to the resurrection of Jesus. Its own existence is the great witness to its faith. And it is important to observe that, even if we had not the documentary evidence of the Pauline epistles as the earliest records of the gospels, and of the Acts of the Apostles, we should still have sufficient proof that the belief in the Resurrection is as old as the church. For the continuance of the church cannot be explained without it. If that faith had not dawned on their slow sad hearts on that Easter morning, a few weeks would have seen them scattered: and if once they had been scattered, as they inevitably would have been, no power could have reunited them, any more than a diamond once shattered can be pieced together again. There would have been no motive and no actors to frame a story of resurrection when once the little company had melted away. The existence of the church depended on their belief that the Lord was risen. In the nature of the case that belief must have followed immediately on his death. It, and it only, reasonably accounts for the facts. And so, over and above apostles, and gospels, and epistles, the church is the great witness, by its very being, to its own immediate and continuous belief in the resurrection of our Lord.

The Resurrection Was a Fact

Again, we may remark that such a belief could not have originated or maintained itself unless it had been true.

Our previous remarks have gone no farther than to establish the belief in the resurrection of Christ, as the basis of primitive Christianity. It is vehemently alleged, and we may freely admit, that the step is a long one from subjective belief to objective reality. But still it is surely perfectly fair to argue that a given belief is of such a nature that it cannot be supposed to rest on anything less solid than a fact; and this is eminently the case in regard to the belief in Christ's resurrection. There have been many attempts on the part of those who reject that belief to account for its existence, and each of them in succession has "had its day, and ceased to be." Unbelief devours its own children remorselessly, and the succession to the throne of anti-Christian skepticism is won, as in some barbarous tribes, by slaying the reigning sovereign. The armies of the aliens turn their weapons against one another, and each new assailant of the historical veracity of the gospels commences operations by showing that all previous assailants have been wrong, and that none of their explanations will hold water.

For instance, we hear nothing now of the coarse old explanation that the story of the Resurrection was a lie, and became current through the conscious imposture of the leaders of the church. And it was high time that such a solution should be laid aside. Who, with half an eye for character, could study the deeds and writings of the apostles, and not feel that, whatever else they were, they were profoundly honest, and as convinced as of their own existence, that they had seen Christ "alive after His passion, by many infallible proofs"? If Paul and Peter and John were conspirators in a trick, then their lives and their words were the most astounding anomaly. Who, either, that had the faintest perception of the forces that sway opinion and frame systems, could believe that the fair fabric of Christian morality was built bubbling up from the very pit of hell? Do men gather grapes of thorns, or figs of thistles? That insolent hypothesis has had its day.

Then when it was discredited, we were told the mythical tendency would explain everything. It showed us how good men could tell lies without knowing it, and how the religious value of an alleged fact in an alleged historical revelation did not in the least depend on its being a fact. And that great discovery, which first converted solid historical Christianity into a gaseous condition, and then caught the fumes in some kind of retort, and professed to hand us them back again improved by the sublimation, has pretty well gone the way of all hypotheses. Myths are not made in three days, or in three years, and no more tie can be allowed for the formation of the myth of the resurrection. What was the church to feed on while the myth was growing? It would have been starved to death long before.

Then, the last new explanation which is gravely put forward, and is the prevailing one now, sustains itself by reference to undeniable facts in the history of religious movements, and of such abnormal attitudes of the mind as modern spiritualism. On the strength of which analogy we are invited to see in the faith of the early Christians in the resurrection of the Lord a gigantic instance of "hallucination." No doubt there have been, and still are, extraordinary instances of its power, especially in minds excited by religious ideas. But we have only to consider the details of the facts in hand to feel that they cannot be accounted for on such a ground.

Do hallucinations lay hold on five hundred people at once? Does a hallucination last for a long country walk, and give rise to protracted conversation? Does hallucination explain the story of Christ eating and drinking before His disciples? The uncertain twilight of the garden might have begotten such an airy phantom in the brain of a single sobbing woman; but the appearances to be explained are so numerous, so varied in character, embrace so many details, appeal to so many of the senses—the ear and hand as well as to the eye —were spread over so long a period, and were simultaneously shared by so large a number, that no theory of such a sort can account for them, unless by impugning the veracity of the records. And then we are back again on the old abandoned ground of deceit and imposture. It sounds plausible to say, Hallucination is a proved cause of many a supposed supernatural event—why not of this? But the plausibility of the solution ceases as soon as you try it on the actual facts in their variety and completeness. It has to be eked out with a length of the fox's skin of deceit before it covers them; and we may confidently assert that such a belief as the belief of the early church in the resurrection of the Lord was never the product either of deceit or of illusion, or of any amalgam of the two.

What new solutions the fertility of unbelief may yet bring forth, and the credulity of unbelief may yet accept, we know not: but we may firmly hold by the faith which breathed new hope and strange joy into that sad band on the first Easter morning, and rejoice with them in the glad wonderful fact that Christ is risen from the dead.

The Joy of the Resurrection

For the message of the resurrection is a message to us as truly as to the heavy-hearted unbelieving men that first received it. We may think for a moment of the joy with which *we* should return from the sepulcher of the risen Savior.

How little these women knew that, as they went back from the grave in the morning twilight, they were the bearers of "great joy which should be to all people!" To them and to the first hearers of their message there would be little clear in the rush of glad surprise, beyond the blessed thought, then He is not gone from us altogether. Sweet visions of the resumption of happy companionship would fill their minds, and it would not be until calmer moments that the stupendous significance of the fact would reveal itself.

Mary's rapturous gesture to clasp Christ by the feet, when the certainty that it was in very deed He, flooded her soul with dazzling light, reveals her first emotion, which no doubt was also the first with them all, "Then we shall have Him with us again, and all the old joy of companionship will be ours once more." Nor were they wrong in thinking so, however little they as yet understood the future manner of their fellowship, or anticipated His leaving them so soon. Nor are we without a share even in that phase of their joy; for the resurrection of Jesus Christ gives us a living Lord for our love, an ever present Companion and Brother for our hearts to hold, even if our hands cannot clasp Him by the feet. A dead Christ might have been the object of faint historical admiration, and the fair statue might have stood amidst others in the halls of the world; but the risen, living Christ can love and be loved, and we too may be glad with the joy of those who have found a heart to rest their hearts upon, and a companionship that can never fail.

As the early disciples learned to reflect upon the fact of Christ's resurrection, its riches unfolded themselves by degrees, and the earliest aspect of its "power" was the light it shed on His person and work. Taught by it, as we have seen, they recognized Him for the Messiah whom they had long expected, and for something more—the Incarnate Son of God. That phase of their joy belongs to us too. If Christ, who made such avowals of His nature as we know He did, and hazarded such assertions of His claims, His personality and His office, as fill the gospels, were really laid in the grave and saw corruption, then the assertions are disproved, the claims unwarranted, the office a figment of His imagination. He may still remain a great teacher, with a tremendous deduction to be made from the worth of His teaching. But all that is deepest in His own words about Himself, and His relation to men, must be sorrowfully put on one side. But if He, after such assertions and claims, rose from the dead, and rising, dieth no more, then for the last time, and in the mightiest tones, the voice that rent the heavens at His baptism and His transfiguration proclaims: "This is My beloved Son; hear ye Him" (Mark 9:11). Our joy in His resurrection is the joy of those to whom He is therein declared to be the Son of God, and who see in Christ risen their accepted Sacrifice, and their ever-living Redeemer.

Such was the earliest effect of the resurrection of Jesus, if we trust the records of apostolic preaching. Then by degrees the joyful thought took shape in the church's consciousness that their Shepherd had gone before them into the dark pen where death pastured his flocks, and had taken it for His own, for the quiet resting-place where He would make them lie down by still waters, and whence He would lead them out to the lofty mountains where His fold should be. The power of Christ's resurrection as the pattern and pledge of ours is the final source of the joy which may fill our hearts as we turn away from that empty sepulcher.

The world has guessed and feared, or guessed and hope, but always guessed and doubted the life beyond. Analogies, poetic adumbrations, probabilities drawn from consciousness and from conscience, from intuition and from anticipation, are but poor foundations on which to build a solid faith. But to those to whom the resurrection of Christ is a fact their own future life is a fact. Here we have a solid certainty, and here alone. The heart says as we lay our dear ones in the grave, "Surely we part not for ever." The conscience says, as it points us to our own evil deeds, "After death the judgment." A deep indestructible instinct prophesies in every breast of a future. But all is vague and doubtful. The one proof of a life beyond the grave is the resurrection of Jesus Christ. Therefore, let us be glad with the gladness of men plucked from a dark abyss of doubt and uncertainty, and planted on the rock of solid certainty; and let us rejoice with joy unspeakable, and laden with a prophetic weight of glory, as we ring out the ancient Easter morning's greeting, "The Lord is risen indeed!"

A Living Hope of the Hereafter

David Martyn Lloyd-Jones (1898-1981) was born in Wales and was taken to London in 1914. There he trained for a medical career and was associated with the famous Dr. Thomas Horder in Harley Street. He abandoned medicine for the gospel ministry, and from 1927 to 1938 he served the Presbyterian Church at Sandfields, Aberavon, Wales. In 1938, he became associate minister with Dr. G. Campbell Morgan at the Westminster Chapel, London; and in 1943, when Morgan retired, Lloyd-Jones succeeded him. His expositions of the Scriptures attracted great crowds wherever he preached. He retired in 1968 to devote his time to writing and limited itinerant ministry. Calvinistic in doctrine, he emphasized the "plight of man and the power of God to save."

This message is reprinted from *Special-Day Sermons for Evangelicals*, edited by Andrew W. Blackwood (Channel Press, Great Neck, New York 1961).

David Martyn Lloyd-Jones

3

A LIVING HOPE OF THE HEREAFTER

> Blessed be the God and Father of our Lord Jesus Christ,
> which according to his abundant mercy hath begotten us
> again unto a lively hope by the resurrection of Jesus Christ
> from the dead, to an inheritance incorruptible, and unde-
> filed, and that fadeth not away, reserved in heaven for us,
> who are kept by the power of God through faith unto sal-
> vation ready to be revealed in the last time (1 Peter 1:3-5;
> read 1:1-25).

AT THE VERY beginning of his letter the apostle Peter bursts
forth into this mighty and magnificent doxology. After a
very brief salutation he suddenly breaks forth in these
thrilling and powerful words. In so doing the apostle was
not doing anything unique. He was doing what all the
early Christians did, what all the writers of the New
Testament epistles invariably do. The moment they
mention the name of our Lord and Savior Jesus Christ
they burst forth into much the same thrilling ascription of
praise. Take the apostle Paul, for example, in the first
chapter of his Epistle to the Ephesians: "Blessed be the
God and Father of our Lord Jesus Christ, who hath blessed
us with all spiritual blessings in heavenly places in Christ"
(Eph. 1:3); and so on to the end of the fourteenth verse of
that wonderful chapter.

The Characteristic of True Christians

That is the great characteristic of the true Christian
always, as it is the great characteristic of the New
Testament, and as it was the characteristic note of the
early church. The early church was characterized by
praises to God, and by a sense of joy. "Blessed be the God
and Father!" That was their note, and as we have seen, it
came out all at once. But that note of praise and joy was
not confined to the early church. If you read the long

history of Christianity you will find that the note of praise and joy has been characteristic of the church in every period of revival. At every time of reformation and renewal this original note has come back, so that the church again has been thrilled with a sense of "wonder, love, and praise." An apostle like Peter, even when he writes to people who at the time are suffering a good deal of trial and tribulation, cannot take up his pen without starting out in this mighty and magnificent manner.

Very well! Before we as Christians go any further let us ask ourselves some obvious questions. Is this the characteristic note of our Christian life and witness? Is this what we feel? Is this our response to the Gospel? Is this our actual experience in the modern world, and in spite of everything awful in the world about us? On this Easter morning, this is surely the most important thing for us to say to ourselves. We claim to be Christians. We make our public profession of faith. But in the last analysis what is the test of it all? Is there within us the spirit that was in the apostle Peter and in the people to whom he wrote?

Of those people the apostle was able to declare: "Wherein ye greatly rejoice, though now for a season, if need be, ye are in heaviness through manifold temptations" (1:6). A little later he wrote about Christ: "Whom not having seen, ye love; in whom, though now ye see him not, yet believing, ye rejoice with joy unspeakable and full of glory" (1:8). Peter said all that about ordinary folk like ourselves. On this Easter morning we meet together claiming to believe this wondrous fact of the resurrection of the Son of God. But the important question is: What is our feeling, what is our reaction, what is our response to this mighty message that we claim to believe?

Can we say that we are like the apostle, and that contemplating it all we have nothing else to exclaim, but that we feel: "Blessed be the God and Father of our Lord Jesus Christ"? If that is our position, the words that we are going to consider will confirm and strengthen us, adding to our joy and assurance. But if we cannot say that honestly, then let us pay heed to what the apostle tells us. Here, fortunately, as is the custom of the inspired writers, he lets us into the secret of why he felt that way himself, why he had to burst forth into this mighty praise, adoration, and thanksgiving.

So let us follow the apostle. With him let us meditate on this wondrous fact of the living hope. In essence he tells us that the Resurrection is central and vital to the whole position of the Christian. Notice the line of thought: "Blessed," says Peter, "blessed be the God and Father of our Lord Jesus Christ, which according to his abundant mercy hath begotten us again unto a lively hope." But how has it all been done? "By the resurrection of Jesus Christ from the dead." That is the center, that is the foundation, that is the thing which makes it all possible, and likewise brings it all to us. Here then is the controlling principle: apart from the resurrection there can be no Christianity. The resurrection of Christ is vital; it is absolutely essential.

Were it not for the resurrection of Christ, the apostle could never have written about the living hope. If you question that, read in the Gospel according to John the beginning of the twenty-first chapter. There after the crucifixion and death of Christ, you see the apostles, Peter among them, utterly downcast and disconsolate, despondent, and despairing, so much so that Peter turned to the others, and said, "I go a-fishing." He felt that he must do something to relieve the tension and the sense of despair. What was it then that transformed him into the "apostle of Hope," who was able to exclaim, "Blessed be the God and Father of our Lord Jesus Christ, which hath begotten us again unto a lively hope"? It was this, the Resurrection!

This truth then is basic and foundational. If a man does not believe in the resurrection of Christ, whatever else he may believe, he has no right to call himself a Christian. The great message that the apostles preached, as you will find it in the Acts of the Apostles, was this: "Jesus and the Resurrection." But for that mighty truth, they would not have preached at all. This was ever their theme: "Jesus and the Resurrection."

The Meaning of the Lively Hope

What is it then that the Resurrection does? Why is it so central and so foundational? For your consideration let me divide into two parts what the apostle here says. The first thing is that the resurrection of Christ gives us "a lively hope." A better translation here would be, "a living hope." If it is living, of course it is lively. A thing that is dead does not move, but if there is life there is liveliness. Why does the apostle trouble to describe it in this way? No doubt he is contrasting it with the vague, the shadowy, and the uncertain. Today there is much that passes for Christian hope, but when you test it by his adjective "living," or "lively," you at once expose it as counterfeit.

What is the message of Easter morning? Is it simply some vague saying that spring has come again, and that after the death of winter there are signs of life? Is the Easter hope something vague and general, belonging only to nature? There are many who tell us that this is all the day can mean to us: that there is always a turn; that you go round the circle of the year, and in time come back to the spring. So we must never despair! That, they assure us, is the message of Easter, something vague, nebulous, unreal.

That is not what Peter is talking about. "Who hath begotten us to a living hope." Something substantial, something certain, something vibrant with life and power. Of course that is essential, he says, because the great thing about this hope is that it enables us to live. As I have already reminded you, the apostle was writing this letter to people who were experiencing a very hard time: "Now for a season, if need be, ye are in heaviness through manifold temptations" (1:6). That is the background of Peter's first epistle. In every chapter he refers much to adversity.

In the second chapter he says, in effect: You are having a hard time but understand this, you are simply "following in his steps, who did no wrong, neither was guile found in his mouth, and when he suffered, he threatened not" (2:22-23a). In the fourth chapter Peter refers to adversity in the time of Noah and the few godly folk left alive in that godless age. Again, in the fourth chapter, the apostle says: "Think it not strange concerning the fiery trial which is to try you, as though some strange thing had happened unto you" (4:12). Don't be surprised! And in the final chapter he leads up to a glorious doxology, with these words at its heart: "after ye have suffered a while" (5:10).

In other words, the New Testament is intensely practical. This is not a story or a fairy tale, not the optimism of the novelist, or the cheeriness of a politician. No, no, this is Christian realism. This does not minimize difficulties, problems, and trials: The whole purpose here is to show that whatever they are, however bad they may be, however dark, ugly, and cruel, it does not really matter to us who believe. We have a "living hope" that can hold us, sustain us, and enable us not only to endure, but to be "more than conquerors." Hence we can look at it all, and in the face of it all, we can smile.

In the eighth chapter of Romans Paul says the same thing: Everything is against us. "We are accounted as sheep for the slaughter." And yet it doesn't really matter! "Nay, in all these things we are more than conquerors through him that loved us" (8:36b-37). This is the living hope. The living hope not only enables a man to go through the very worst that hell can produce against him. This lively hope also enables him to do so with assurance, and with a sense of triumph. This is the apostle Peter's message to us at Easter time: "We have been begotten again unto a lively hope."

How does the Resurrection accomplish all this? As we go along from point to point I trust that we are examining ourselves. Do you now have within you this assurance that you are "more than conqueror"? In your personal life, in your married life at home, in your business or profession, in the group to which you belong, and in the whole world as it is today, what is your reaction to your circumstances? Does this mighty fact of the Resurrection give you a sense of certainty and of assurance, of triumph and of joy? Are you "rejoicing in your tribulations," and lifted up above them all, so that you can look at them all and exclaim: "Blessed be the God and Father of our Lord Jesus Christ"?

Here then for us is the important matter. To us who believe in the Resurrection, does it bring us today this "living," this "lively hope"?

Here we must divide our answer into two sections. In the first place the Resurrection does this because of what it did to the Lord Jesus Christ Himself. That is the starting point of faith. That is what I meant at the beginning by emphasizing as the whole basis of Christian faith the fact that the resurrection of Christ is literal. What I mean by literal fact is that the apostle is not merely referring to the truth that the Lord Jesus who had been crucified on Friday was still alive in the spirit realm. What the apostle refers to is that the Lord Jesus literally came out of the grave; that He came out of the grave in His body; that the body which had been crucified on Friday, which had been taken down when He died, and which had been placed in the sepulcher, that very same body had come out of the tomb. Hence the empty tomb lies at the basis of all our Easter hopes.

I am emphasizing this, of course, for a very good reason. Probably you have been reading, as I have been reading in various newspapers, articles about the Resurrection, about Easter, and about related truths. Doubtless you have found that nearly all of them refer only to the fact of "survival." That of course holds true, but it is totally inadequate. We are not here today merely to celebrate survival of personality. That is not the message of Easter. The survival of personality was believed in before Easter, and is believed in today by many who are not Christians at all.

No, no! The specific message of Easter is this, that our Lord and Savior Jesus Christ was crucified and was buried; that He was raised from the dead in His body; that He came out of the tomb a complete personality, with His body and everything else; and that He left His grave empty. Hence the details that appear in the twentieth chapter of John's Gospel, as in the other three. How careful they are to note that the napkin which had been round His head lay in a position different from that of the other grave clothes. The sacred writers give such details to show that the Resurrection is literal, historical fact. The record is so minute as to satisfy any detective who wishes to investigate. For the great fact of the resurrection of our Lord's body and evidence is as definite and certain as for any other event in the long history of the human race.

The Meaning of the Resurrection

Once again, Christ was raised by God the Father. This we learn from our text, as later from verse twenty-three, and elsewhere in the Epistles. What does this mean? Looking at it in the light of the New Testament, the Christian way of looking at the Resurrection. Here is the Eternal Son of God, the Second Person in the blessed Holy Trinity. Having from eternity been in the bosom of the Father, and having spent His eternal existence in that ineffable glory, at a given point He entered into time. What for? What did He do? He took unto Himself our human nature. He entered into this world, into our realm of sin and death. As the apostle Paul says, Christ "was made of a woman, made under the law."

These things you cannot understand, except theologically. They mean that He who was divine and glorious also became human and lowly. "The Word was made flesh" (John 1:14a). Not only was He born of a woman. He was also "made under the law." As a Man amongst men He came into this world of sin. He did not cease to be God, but in addition He also became Man, a complete Man. He had a human body, such as you and I have, with bodily infirmities. There was in Him no element of sin, but there were infirmities. They appear whenever you read the accounts of His life in the pages of the four Gospels. And as a human being He was subject to temptation. As God He could not be tempted with evil (James 1:13), but as Man He not only could be, He was so tempted. He "was in all points tempted like as we are, yet without sin" (Heb. 4:15b). When He came into this world He identified Himself with us fully.

All the opposition of the devil and his followers, all the malignity of hell, was turned upon Him. Those enemies of God, those infernal powers, were determined to destroy

Him, because they knew that He was the Son of God. In the Gospels you find the demons recognizing Him and begging Him to leave them alone. Indeed, the entire forces of hell were massed against Him. They were determined to destroy Him, and thus to thwart the whole purpose of God connected with His coming. Finally, we see this conspiracy of evil coming to its climax. Not only were all those powers set against Him as the Son of God. At last we see Him being led to the Cross, there to be nailed, and to die.

What is happening at the Cross? According to the Scriptures, as Peter puts it in his second chapter here, God was laying our sins on Him, "who his own self bare our sins in his own body on the tree" (2:24a). Or as Paul puts it, God "hath made him to be sin for us, who knew no sin, that we might be made the righteousness of God in him" (2 Cor. 5:21). What does this mean? It means that there on the Cross of Calvary's hill all that the Law has to say against sin was said. All the punishment that the Law metes out upon sin and guilt, evil and shame, was poured out upon Him.

That is what was happening at the Cross. All the righteous demands of God's Law were being fulfilled. All the consequences of sin were being poured out upon Him. That was what he was doing, what He had come to earth to do. Sin led to His death. Sin was the cause of His crucifixion. "Without shedding of blood there is no remission" of sins (Heb. 9:22b). And so He died. His body was taken down and buried in the grave. Then came the momentous fact of the Resurrection. This is the truth, says Peter, in effect, that thrills me and grips me, moving me to cry out in wonder and adoration. Christ did not remain in the grave. He was brought out of it, unscathed and conquering. He appeared to His chosen followers, ascended into heaven, and again took His seat in the everlasting glory.

That is the first and the most important thing for us to grasp. But what does it mean? Let us listen to the exposition of it by Paul in his Epistle to the Romans. In the sixth chapter he puts the truth like this: "Christ, being raised from the dead, dieth no more; death hath no more dominion over him. For in that he died, he died unto sin once; but in that he liveth, he liveth unto God" (6:9-10). Do you get the significance to that? It is the heart of the Gospel. Note that word, "once"! "In that he died, he died once." Now, says Paul, "death hath no more dominion over him." Once on earth death did have dominion over Christ.

That is the whole marvel of the Incarnation and all that the Son of God did on earth, with all that was done to Him. He subjected Himself to all that the Law had to say about sin. He was "made of a woman, made under the law," the Law against sin. Not that He ever sinned, or was ever sinful. But as a part of His identification with us He took His place at our side. For that reason He submitted to baptism: "Suffer it to be so now, for thus it becometh us to fulfill all righteousness" (Matt. 3:15). In order to deal with the problem of our sins He had come into the world. He became one with us. He was under the Law, the Law that condemns. The Law condemned Him because of our sins. "He died unto sin once."

He died once, but no more, forever! The Resurrection is the great announcement of the momentous fact that Christ has finished the work He came to do. He is no longer "under the law;" He is back in glory. Why? Because He has done everything that the Law could demand. Now the Law has exhausted itself upon Him, and He will die "no more." He need not have died at all. Deliberately He came into the realm of sin and death, in order to deliver us from it all. Now He dieth "no more; death hath no more dominion over him!" That is the meaning of the Resurrection. He has gone back into the realm above and beyond sin and law and death. He has conquered that entire realm, and He has returned to the glory from whence He came. That is the meaning of the Resurrection.

The Union With the Living Christ

That is the basic fact about the Resurrection. But that is not all. The apostle says that because of what happened to Him on the Cross you and I have this "lively hope."

Yes, but likewise because of what has happened to us. "What has happened to us?" says someone. "What do you mean?" The answer comes from the words of the apostle: "Blessed be the God and Father of our Lord Jesus Christ, which according to His abundant mercy hath begotten us again unto a lively hope." Notice that phrase, "begotten us again." What does it mean? In the twenty-third verse of this chapter Peter uses exactly the same word: "Being born [or begotten] again, not of corruptible seed, but of incorruptible, by the word of God, which liveth and abideth forever."

God "hath begotten us again." We have been "born again unto a living hope." This is the very term that the apostle uses. What does this mean? It means that the Christian not merely believes in Christ as the Son of God, and believes that He was raised from the dead. Of course he believes that! You cannot be a Christian without believing that. But that is not the whole truth about the Christian's beliefs. The Christian is a man who knows that he has been regenerated unto a living hope. He has been born again unto a lively hope.

What does this mean? Regeneration means "new life." We who believe have been "born again unto a lively hope." Until you are born again, you will never have this living hope. The natural man does not have it. He is without Christ, "having no hope, and without God in the world" (Eph. 2:12c). The only man who has this living hope, the only one who can smile in the face of death, is the man who has been regenerated, begotten again, born again. Someone asks, "How did it happen?" The answer is, "By the resurrection of Jesus Christ from the dead." We are regenerated, born again, by the agency of the Holy Spirit, through the medium of Christ's Resurrection from the dead. Born again unto a lively hope!

How does all that come about? In many ways it is the most remarkable of all the Christian doctrines. It is the doctrine of our Union with Christ. We are one with Him. What happened to Him happened to us. Again let Paul expound the doctrine, in Romans six. "Shall we continue in sin, that grace may abound? God forbid," says the apostle. "How shall we, that are dead to sin, live any longer therein? Know ye not, that so many of us as were baptized into Jesus Christ were baptized into his death? Therefore we are buried with him by baptism into death, that like as Christ was raised up from the dead by the glory of the Father, even so we also should walk in newness of life. For if we have been planted together in the likeness of his death, we shall be also in the likeness of His resurrection" (6:1-5).

Then the apostle goes on: "Knowing that Christ being raised from the dead dieth no more; death hath no more dominion over him. . . . Likewise reckon ye also yourselves to be dead indeed unto sin, but alive unto God through Jesus Christ our Lord" (6:9, 11). This is the truth that he utters everywhere. Listen to it in Colossians: "Ye are dead, and your life is hid with Christ in God" (3:3). Also in Ephesians: "You hath he quickened, who were dead in trespasses and sins. . . . But God, who is rich in mercy . . . even when ye were dead in sins, hath quickened us together with Christ . . . and hath raised us up together, and made us sit together in heavenly places in Christ Jesus" (2:1, 4-6). All that comes to pass because of the Resurrection.

This is how a man gets the living hope. It comes because he is joined to Christ. He is in this blessed state of union with Christ, so that what happened to the Lord Jesus also happens to him. Christ and His people are one. He is the Head; we are the body. When He died, we died. When He was buried in a grave, we were buried with Him. When He arose, we arose. So the apostle says that as He is dead to the law, dead to sin, and dead to death, so are we! A Christian is a man who can say: "Death has no dominion over me!" As a Christian he at last "falls on sleep." He has already passed through what death really means. Because Christ has tasted death for him (Heb. 2; 9:9), he himself will never "taste death." He is alive with Christ, now and for ever more. He has "begotten again [regenerated] unto a lively hope by the resurrection of Jesus Christ from the dead." That is how it all happens.

The Resurrection of the Believer's Body

What does this all lead to? The apostle Peter says that the Resurrection leads to a "living hope." What then is the living hope? It is "an inheritance incorruptible, and undefiled, and that fadeth not away, reserved in heaven for you" (1 Peter 1:4). What is the hope of the Christian this morning? It is not merely survival, not simply immortality. Let me remind you again that before Christ ever came into this world men in Greece believed in human survival after death. In order to believe in the Resurrection you need not fall back on the phenomena of Spiritism. If you do that, you are denying the Resurrection. This was not merely some spirit making an appearance. This was the body that had been crucified, itself risen and glorified and appearing to certain chosen people. The message of Easter morning is not merely survival, not simply that we shall go on living after we die. The Easter hope is something infinitely beyond that.

What is it? It is essentially this: the resurrection of the body. Our spirits, as we have seen, are already resurrected. We have been "begotten again," "born anew," "regenerated." A man who is a Christian is one who is already renewed in spirit. Yes, but here we learn that he shall also be renewed in his body. It means, says Peter, that in heaven we shall enter into this inheritance, and that we shall enter into it as complete personalities. The hope of the Christian is not that he will go to some vague, shadowy realm, some sort of Elysium. No, forget all that, and all the other nonsense of Spiritism. The resurrection of the believer is real. It comes to the complete man—not to a spirit floating in some atmosphere—but to the complete man, body, soul and spirit, renewed and glorified, and ready to enter into his everlasting inheritance. This is the living hope to which we have been begotten: "To an inheritance incorruptible, and undefiled, and that fadeth not away, reserved in heaven for you, who are kept by the power of God through faith unto salvation ready to be revealed in the last time" (1 Peter 1:4, 5).

What does all of this mean? It means that God once made this world perfect, a paradise. In it He put a man, who was perfect. And God is not going to be satisfied until all that has been restored. Hence I do not spend Easter morning in protesting against atomic and hydrogen bombs! I have a message that is infinitely higher. This old world is doomed. It is a sinful world, an awful world, and man can never make it a good world. He can protest, he can march, he can pass acts of Parliament. But he can never make the world good, because the sin is in himself. When he lived in paradise, he turned it into a place of shame.

O No! Man can never put this world right, but God can, and He will. "Blessed be the God and Father of our Lord Jesus Christ, which according to his abundant mercy hath begotten us again unto a lively hope by the resurrection of Jesus Christ from the dead." A lively hope of what? That this old world is going to be renewed! The regeneration is going to take place in the entire cosmos. When? When the Lord Jesus Christ comes again in glory. The Lord Jesus Himself tells of "the regeneration when the Son of man shall sit in the throne of his glory" (Matt. 19:28*b*). That is the Christian message. He has triumphed over all His enemies. He is risen, and He is seated at the right hand of God. What is He doing? He is waiting until His enemies become His footstool (Ps. 110:1). Then He will come back to earth again as "King of kings and Lord of lords." He will destroy out of existence all that is sinful and vile, ugly and foul. He will renew the whole creation, and bring in His glorious kingdom. The City of God, the New Jerusalem, will descend, and God will make His tabernacle amongst men.

This is what the living hope means to us. If we are Christians we shall be there. Not as vague spirits floating in a nameless sea of existence. No—but in this body as glorified, delivered from all vestiges of sin and shame, weakness and wildness. You will be identified as yourself. You will be in a glorified body. "Our citizenship is in heaven," says Paul to the Philippians, "whence also we wait for the Savior, the Lord Jesus Christ, who shall change this our vile body, that it may be fashioned like unto his glorious body, according to the working of that mighty power by which he is able to subdue even all things unto himself" (3:20-21).

That is what the inheritance means. It is coming, and I am looking forward to it. I know now that I have been born again unto this hope by the resurrection of Jesus Christ from the dead. Oh, the blessedness of this knowledge! You and I dwell in an old world that may at any moment be blown into nothing. Does that depress you? Does the idea monopolize all your thought? Is that the one thing always on your tongue? If so, I do not hesitate to assert that you are a very poor Christian, if a Christian at all.

By faith the Christian sees this old world after the coming "regeneration." Meanwhile he has his eyes fixed on another land. What does he behold about it? It is "incorruptible;" it will be "undefiled;" it will never "fade away." Nothing from outside will be able to affect this "incorruptible" realm. The devil and all his cohorts, with all their diabolical powers, will have been cast into the lake of destruction, whatever that may mean, and there they will be helpless. Nothing evil or sinful will enter into it, for it will be "undefiled." And it will never "fade away." It will go on and on, in everlasting glory! That is our Easter hope. That is our Christian inheritance. That is the truth into which you as a Christian have been born again. That is the truth to sustain you in all your trials.

So this morning as I look over this evil, sinful world it does not depress me, because I expect from it nothing better. Whatever may be going against me, whatever may be happening in my own body, this is what I must expect, because of sin. But though I die, I shall rise again. I shall see Him face to face. I shall see Him as He is, and I shall be like Him, like Him in a body glorified, with every power renewed. And I shall be living in a realm that is incorruptible and undefiled, a realm that can never fade away.

The Message of Easter Morning

That is the living hope of the Resurrection. That is the message of this Easter morning. And that hope is absolutely safe and secure. The Resurrection itself guarantees it all. Every enemy has been destroyed. Christ has conquered them every one. In the Epistle to the Hebrews the inspired author states all this clearly. Having written that God has put all things under Christ, the apostle goes on to say: "But now we see not yet all things put under Him." "I agree," the apostle says, in effect, "but we see Jesus, who was made a little lower than the angels for the suffering of death, crowned with glory and honor" (2:8c-9).

Christ is our Forerunner (Heb. 6:20). He has gone to prepare a place for us, and He will come again to receive us unto Himself (John 14:2b-3). We shall "reign with him as kings and priests." We shall "judge the world." We shall even "judge angels." That is Christ's guarantee, and nothing can stop it. Can death? Of course not, for He has already conquered death! Can the devil? No, Christ has vanquished the devil. Can hell? No, no! "O death, where is thy sting? O grave, where is thy victory? . . . Thanks be to God, which giveth us the victory through our Lord Jesus Christ"! (1 Cor. 15:55, 57). The resurrection of Christ announces that He has conquered every enemy. He has vanquished every foe. He has risen triumphant from the grave. Neither death nor life, neither hell nor anything else, can prevent or delay the coming of His Kingdom in all its glory. He alone is King of kings and Lord of lords.

Christian people, do you have this living hope? Are your eyes fixed upon the inheritance that He has purchased for you? Is there within you at this moment something that is crying out—it may be feebly—crying out from the hopelessness and the despair, the sin and the shame, the failure and the disgrace, the disease and the death of this life—crying out triumphantly the words of our text?

"Blessed be the God and Father of our Lord Jesus Christ, which according to his abundant mercy hath begotten us again unto a lively hope by the resurrection of Christ from the dead, to an inheritance incorruptible and undefiled, and that fadeth not away, reserved in heaven for you." Reserved for you by the very same God who also keeps us, gives us wisdom and power, with ability to endure and to triumph in spite of everything. "Blessed be the God and Father of our Lord Jesus Christ!"

Easter Joy

Henry Parry Liddon (1829-1890) belonged to the High Church school of the Anglican Church. Ordained in 1853, he served in two brief pastorates and as vice-principal of a school. He moved to Oxford and there preached to large crowds at St. Mary's and Christ Church. He is perhaps best known for his Bampton Lectures, *The Divinity of Our Lord and Savior Jesus Christ*. From 1870 until his death, he was canon of St. Paul's Cathedral, London, which he sought to make into an Anglican preaching center to rival Charles Spurgeon's Metropolitan Tabernacle.

This sermon comes from *Easter in St. Paul's*, published in 1907 by Longmans, Green, and Co., London. It has been slightly abridged for this volume.

Henry Parry Liddon

4

EASTER JOY

Thou hast turned my heaviness into joy: Thou hast put off my sackcloth, and girded me with gladness (Psalm 30:12).

HERE IS DESCRIBED a change, complete, and more or less sudden, from sadness to joy. David has escaped a danger which had brought him very near to death; and now he is thankful and exultant. His words are in keeping with what Christians feel, as they pass from the last days of Holy Week into the first hours of Easter. If Easter is associated predominantly with any one emotion, it is with that of joy. When Mary Magdalene and the other Marys had heard the words of the angel of the Lord, "they departed quickly from the sepulcher, with fear and great joy" (Matt. 28:8). When, on the evening of Easter Day, Jesus stood in the midst of the assembled disciples, and showed them His Hands and His Feet, their joy was too great for the steady exercise of their understanding: "they believed not for joy, and wondered" (Luke 24:40, 41). In these first hours of ecstatic bewilderment, as John says, "the disciples were glad when they saw the Lord" (John 20:20). Was it not His Own promise of a joy which would be beyond the reach of outward circumstance, that had now become true? "Verily, verily, I say unto you, That ye shall weep and lament, but the world shall rejoice"—that was the hour of Calvary—"and ye shall be sorrowful, but your sorrow shall be turned into joy" (John 16:20)—that was to be the radiance of Easter. "A woman when she is in travail hath sorrow, because her hour is come: but as soon as she is delivered of the child, she remembereth no more the anguish, for joy that a man is born into the world. And ye now therefore have sorrow; but I will see you again, and your heart shall rejoice, and your joy no man taketh from you" (John 16:21, 22).

51

And thus, ever since, the church of Christ has labored to make the Easter festival, beyond all others, the feast of Christian joy. All that nature and art could furnish has been summoned to express, so far as outward things may, this overmastering emotion of Christian souls worshiping at the tomb of their Risen Lord. All the deliverances of God's ancient people, from Egypt, from Assyria, from Babylon, are but rehearsals of the great deliverance of all on the Resurrection morning; and each prophet and psalmist that heralds any of them, sounds in Christian ears some separate note of the Resurrection hymn. "Sing unto the Lord, for He hath triumphed gloriously" (Exod. 15:21); or, "He hath broken the gates of brass, and smitten the bars of iron in sunder" (Ps. 107:16); or, "The Lord awaked as one out of sleep, and like a giant refreshed with wine" (Ps. 78:65); or, "This is the day which the Lord hath made, we will rejoice and be glad in it" (Ps. 118:24)— these, and many other passages, referred originally to some event in Jewish history, and yet are felt to receive their highest fulfillment and interpretation when they are uttered by Christian hearts on the Easter festival. And this, the joy which fills the soul of the believing church on Easter day, has some sort of echo in the world outside; so that those who sit loosely to our faith and hope, and who worship rarely, if ever, before our altars, yet feel that good spirits are somehow in order on Easter morning. For their sakes, as for our own, let us try to take the emotion to pieces, as we find it in a Christian soul; let us ask why it is so natural for Christians to say, this day, with David, "Thou hast turned my heaviness into joy: Thou hast put off my sackcloth, and girded me with gladness."

Joy Experienced by Christ Himself

The first reason, then, for this Easter joy is the triumph and satisfaction enjoyed by our Lord Himself. Certainly it is now more than eighteen hundred years since He died and rose. But we Christians are well assured that He is alive; that He is reigning on His throne in heaven, yet also invisibly with us on earth, and perfectly well aware of all that is passing both within our souls and without them. Yes! eighteen centuries have gone; yet, year by year, we follow Him, step by step, through all the stages of His sufferings and death. We sympathize reverently with the awful sorrows of our adorable Lord and Friend; and thus we enter, in some far-off way, into the sense of triumph, unspeakable and sublime, which follows beyond it. It is His triumph; that is the first consideration; His triumph, who was but now so cruelly insulted and tortured; His, whom they buffeted and spat upon, and mocked and derided, and nailed to the wood, and laid in the sepulcher. It is all over now; His enemies have done their best or their worst; and He has swept it all aside, since, now that the hour has come, by a single motion of His majestic will, He is risen. And we, as we kneel before Him, think, first of all, of Him. It is His joy which inspires ours; it turns our heaviness into joy, and puts off our sorrow and girds us with gladness.

Do I say, This is the case? Perhaps it were more prudent to say, that it ought to be. For in truth the habit of getting out of and forgetting our miserable selves in the absorbing sense of beauty and magnificence of God, belongs rather to ancient than to modern Christianity. Few things are more striking in the early Christian mind, taken as a whole, than its power of escaping from self into the thought and presence of God. To these old Christians God was all, man nothing, or well-nigh nothing. They delighted to dwell on everything that He had told them about Himself, about each one of His attributes, each one of His acts, simply because it was His, and without reference to the question whether it had any or what bearing upon their own lives and need. Theirs was a disinterested interest in God; and to them our Lord's resurrection was, in the first place, of commanding moment, because it meant His glory and triumph, whatever else it might mean for them.

With us moderns the case is somewhat otherwise. We value God, if the truth must be spoken, at least in many cases, not for His Own sake, but for ours. Perhaps, without knowing it, we have drunk deeply into the subjective temper, as it is called, of our time; the temper which assumes that truth only exists so far as we can measure it, or as it exists for us; the temper which practically, like the old sophist in Plato, makes man the measure of all things. With us of today it is too often assumed that the human mind is the center, not merely of human thought, but of universal being. And thus God, the one self-existent Cause of all that is, is banished to a distant point on the circumference of our imaginary universe. Men carry this temper unconsciously into their religion. And thus our first question, in presence of a great truth like the Resurrection, is too often, not, What is its intrinsic importance? but, What interest has it for me?

Look at a modern hymn: it is, as a rule, full of man; full of his wants, his aspirations, his anticipations, his hopes, his fears; full of his religious self, if you will, but still of himself. Read an ancient hymn: it is, as a rule, full of God, of His awful nature; of His wonderful attributes; full of the Eternal Son, of His acts, His sufferings, His triumph, His majesty. Certainly ancient Christianity did justice to the needs and moods of the soul; just as in the Psalms we find the soul's several moods of hope and fear, of penitence and exultation, so abundantly provided for. We often hear even religious people express something like impatience with the great Psalms, which describe God's relations with nature, or His dealings with His people Israel; an impatience grounded on the fact that they think those Psalms only of real interest which enable them to say something to God about themselves. Surely, my friends, we moderns have lost something, nay much, in this matter, by comparison with the early church of Christ; and thus I may have said too much just now, when I took it for granted that the joy of our Lord would be our first reason for rejoicing on Easter Day. Be it yours to show that my misgiving is unwarranted. You know that pure sympathy with an earthly friend's happiness leaves altogether out of consideration the question whether it contributes anything to your own; and in like manner endeavor to say today to your Heavenly Friend: "It is because Thou, Lord Jesus, hast vanquished Thine enemies, hast overcome death, and hast entered into Thy glory, that Thou hast turned my Lenten 'heaviness into joy, and put off my sackcloth, and girded me with gladness'."

Joy Inspired by Confidence in Christian Truth

But, having said this, note, secondly, that Easter joy is inspired by the sense of confidence with which Christ's resurrection from the dead invigorates our grasp of Christian truth.

The understanding, be sure, has its joy, no less than the heart; and a keen sense of intellectual joy is experienced when we succeed in resting truth, or any part of it, on a secure basis. This is what the old Roman poet meant by saying that the man was really happy who had attained to know the causes of things. And no one who has been thrown into close relations with men engaged in the eager pursuit of any branch of knowledge, can mistake the depth and reality of this kind of satisfaction. The chemist who has at last explained the known effect of a particular drug, by laying bare, upon analysis, an hitherto undiscovered property in it; the historian who has been enabled to show that the conjecture of years rests on the evidence of a trustworthy document; the mathematician on whom has flashed the formula which solves some problem that has long haunted and eluded him; the anatomist who has been able to refer what he had hitherto regarded as an abnormal occurrence to the operation of a recognized law;—these men know what joy is. This joy of the understanding at coming into felt contact with some truth underlying that which it has hitherto grasped, wins for it a new vigor and buoyancy, enhances its present sense of life, and is full of hope and promise for the time to come.

Now, akin to the joy of students and workers is the satisfaction of a Christian when he steadily dwells on the resurrection of our Lord Jesus Christ. During large tracts of time we Christians think naturally and mainly of truths or duties, which, however important, are not the foundations of other truths. The Christian creed is like a tower which rears towards heaven its windows and pinnacles in successive stages of increasing gracefulness. We lavish our admiration first on this detail of it, and then on that; and, while we thus study and admire, we dwell continuously in its upper stories, till at last perhaps a grave question occurs or is suggested to us. What does it all rest upon? What is the foundation-fact on which this structure has been reared in all its audacious and fascinating beauty? What is the fact, if there be any, the removal of which would be fatal to the edifice? And the answer is that our Lord's resurrection from the dead is one such fact. It is a foundation on which all truth in the Christian creed, that is distinctively Christian, and not merely Theistic, really rests. Our Lord pointed to it as the certificate of His mission. He rebuked indeed the temper which made men ask whether He could show a sign of having a mission from above: but He granted the request. The prophet Jonah was the type of the Son of Man: "As Jonah was three days and three nights in the whale's belly, so would the Son of Man be three days and three nights in the heart of the earth" (Matt. 12:40).

The earliest sermons of the apostles were almost entirely concerned with Christ's resurrection. As we read them in the Acts it might seem that the Resurrection was the only Christian doctrine. The prophecies which it fulfilled; the consequences to which it pointed; above all, the reality of the fact itself, of which those first preachers were witnesses: this was the subject of the earliest preaching of the apostles of Christ. And why did they dwell so persistently on the Resurrection? Why did they not say more about our Lord's atoning death, or the power of His example, or the drift and character of His moral teaching, or the means of grace with which He has endowed His church? Why, but because, before building the superstructure in the hearts of believers, it was necessary to lay the foundation deep and firm. If it was true that Christ had risen, then the faith of Christendom, in all its vast significance, would be seen, step by step, but surely, to follow; whereas, "if Christ be not risen," as said one of themselves, "our preaching is vain, your faith is also vain" (1 Cor. 15:14).

Here, then, in the resurrection of Christ, we have a solid fact on which the Christian faith securely rests, both as a whole, and in its most vital parts. Does our Lord say that hereafter we shall see the Son of Man sitting on the right hand of power, and coming in the clouds of heaven? If the speaker were a being whose life is conditioned as our own, such language could, at best, be regarded as an extravagant illusion. But if He really rose from the dead, He evidently is a Being of another order than we, and this and much more is possible. Does He speak of giving His Life as a ransom for many; of His blood being shed for the remission of sins? This, again, would be unintelligible or intolerable in an ordinary man; but it is clear that the death of One who resumed His life after His life had been wrung out of Him by a death of torture, may well have consequences beyond our calculation. Does He say that He and the Father are one thing; that to have seen Him is to have seen the Father; that all men should honor the Son—that is, Himself—even as they honor the Father; that unless men would eat His flesh and drink His blood, they would have no true life in them? Ah! what must have been the verdict of the human conscience upon such language as this, if the speaker, after an ignominious execution, had rotted in his grave? Whereas, in view of the considerations which we have had before us, an apostle exclaims that Christ was "declared to be the Son of God with power, by the resurrection from the dead" (Rom. 1:4).

Yes; it is here, beside the empty tomb of the risen Jesus, that Christian faith feels itself on the hard rock of fact; here we break through the tyranny of matter and sense, and rise with Christ into the immaterial world; here we put a term to the enervating alternation of guesses and doubts which prevails elsewhere, and we reach the frontier of the absolutely certain; here, as we kneel in deep thankfulness, and the Christian creed in all its beauty and in all its coherent truth opens out before us, we hear, it may be, as did His beloved apostle, His voice from heaven, "I am He that liveth, and was dead, and behold, I am alive for evermore, and have the keys of hell and of death" (Rev. 1:18). And we can but answer, Truly, Lord Jesus, by Thy resurrection Thou hast turned my heaviness into joy: Thou hast put off my sackcloth, and girded me with gladness.

Joy Brought About by Future Resurrection Hope

But there is a third reason for Easter joy, which must be briefly touched on, before we close.

As a man gets on in life, he finds his deepest human interests transferred, one after another, to a sphere beyond that of sense and time. One after another they are withdrawn, the friends of our childhood, the friends of our manhood, the friends of our riper years. One after another they reach the brink; there is hesitation, it may be, perhaps, for a moment; it seems that they might return. But the hour strikes; and they part. They join the company of the dead! All here remains as it was, at least for a while; the home in which they dwelt, the haunts they frequented, the enterprises in which they were engaged, the faces they loved. All these remain; but they—they are gone! They have disappeared beyond recall; their bodies indeed, we know, lie beneath the sod, a prey to corruption and the worm; but their souls, their spirits, themselves, that which flashed through the eye, that which was felt in the manner, in the tone of the voice, as well as in the thought and action,—where is it? Has it then become absorbed into some sea of life, in which all personality, and with it all consciousness, perishes? Or has it sunk back, after a momentary flicker, into an abyss of nothing, now that the material framework, whose energy it was, is withdrawn?

There is no occasion here to review the arguments by which wise and good men, living in pagan darkness, but making the most of such light as reason and conscience could give them, have attained to belief in the immortality of the soul. We know that their guess or speculation, whichever we deem it, is a solemn certainty. But we know also that it is only half the truth. Man is not merely a spiritual being; he is also an animal organism: and if his spiritual part were to be isolated for an eternity; wrenched away for ever from the sense and framework, in which it has been lodged since the first moment of its existence, then man would be no longer the same being; he would be unrecognizable even by himself. For the spirit strikes its roots deep into the animal organism; indeed this intimate relation between them is the element of truth on which materialism fixes, that it may thence infer its degrading falsehood that man has no purely spiritual being at all. And thus it is that when the gospel brought life and immortality to light, it did this thoroughly. It unveiled the immortality of man in his completeness; the immortality of his spiritualized but still-existing body, as well as the immortality of his soul.

We may then hope to meet our friends, those whom we have loved long since and lost a while not as formless, unrecognizable shades, but with the features, the expressions which they wore on earth. "For if we believe that Jesus died, and rose again, even so them also which sleep in Jesus shall God bring with Him" (1 Thess. 4:14). His resurrection is the model as well as the warrant of our own. Nay more: "All men shall rise with their bodies." In that future world there will, we know, be shadows, dark, impenetrable, unchanging. But there will also be joy unspeakable and full of glory. And if they whom we call the dead know anything of what is passing here on earth; if, as has been supposed by great Christian divines, they see in the Eternal Word, as in a mirror, the reflection of all that happens in this world of sense, from which they have been separated by death, then we may believe that the Easter Festival is for them too, in whatever measure, an occasion of rejoicing, and that the happiness of the church on earth is responded to from beyond the veil. To them, at any rate, our thoughts involuntarily turn, in these moments of rare and thankful joy; they live again now in our memories, though years should have passed since they were withdrawn from our sight; and, as we look forward to the hour when we, unworthy but repentant, through redeeming grace and mercy, shall join them; and beneath the throne of our risen Lord shall again behold the features which we have loved best on earth, can we but exclaim, with deep thankfulness, Thou, O Jesus, hast by Thy resurrection "turned my heaviness into joy: Thou hast put off my sackcloth, and girded me with gladness" (Ps. 30:11).

Resurrection

Henry ("Harry") Allan Ironside (1878-1951) was born in Toronto, Canada, raised in California, and began preaching when he was converted at the age of fourteen. He had no formal training for the ministry but devoted himself to reading and studying of the Bible. His early associations were with the Salvation Army, but then he identified with the Plymouth Brethren and became one of their most beloved itinerant Bible teachers. From 1930 to 1948, he pastored the Moody Church in Chicago. He wrote more than sixty books, many of which are collections of messages given at Moody Church and various conferences.

This message is from *Great Words of the Gospel,* a series of messages given at Moody Church and published by Moody Press in 1944.

5

RESURRECTION

He preached unto them Jesus, and the resurrection . . .
And the times of this ignorance God winked at; but now
commandeth all men everywhere to repent: because he
hath appointed a day, in the which he will judge the world
in righteousness by that man whom he hath ordained;
whereof he hath given assurance unto all men, in that he
hath raised him from the dead (Acts 17:18, 30, 31).

APART FROM THE great fact of the resurrection of our Lord
Jesus Christ from the dead we would have no gospel to
preach. By "resurrection" we do not mean that our Lord's
spirit continued to live after His body died, but that He
was actually raised from the dead by the glory of the
Father, and came forth from the tomb in the very same
body that had been impaled on Calvary's cross. In that
body, now glorified, He sits at God's right hand, and in
that same body He is coming again as the Judge of both
living and dead—the saved and the lost. This is what is
emphasized for us in the seventeenth chapter of the Acts
of the Apostles.

The entire passage, beginning with verse 16, is of
tremendous interest, but I have no thought of attempting
to explain it all, though I hope you will read it carefully at
your leisure, if you are not thoroughly familiar with it, for
it is undoubtedly one of the finest examples of a preacher's
eloquence that we have anywhere in the Bible.

Paul appears here at his best, from the human
standpoint, but he also speaks as a divinely inspired
servant of Christ. Of Apollos we read elsewhere that he
was an eloquent man and mighty in the Scriptures, and it
is very evident from this sample sermon that Paul was a
man of the same stamp; although on the other hand he
did not particularly cultivate what was simply rhetorical,
lest the Cross of Christ should be made of none effect.

But it was quite in keeping with his principle of being "made all things to all men," that, when he stood on Mars' Hill, the very center of culture of the Greek world, he should meet those

Proud Attic Philosophers

on their own ground. So far as culture was concerned, he was every whit their equal, combining a thorough acquaintance with their literature, history and customs, with a deep knowledge of the Word of God to which they were strangers. Thus he gave them that day a new and arresting message such as they had never heard before, and possibly many were destined never to hear again.

Notice some of the circumstances. Paul was waiting in Athens for several of his fellow servants, who had returned to Thessalonica to find out how the newborn Christians there were getting along. As he wandered about the city, his spirit was deeply stirred, for he saw everywhere the evidences of idolatry. They worshiped everything in Athens, in fact an ancient philosopher once said, "In Athens it is easier to find a god than a man." There were images on every street corner, over every doorway, in every courtyard, found in every store, and every dwelling house. Turn where you would, you were confronted by these

Signs of Pagan Darkness

and Paul, as he walked those streets, knew that the things the Gentiles sacrificed were sacrificed to demons and not to God; he knew that he was probably the only man in the city who had a knowledge of the true and living God and of His Son, the Lord Jesus Christ; and yet for the time being he saw no opportunity to give his message in a public way.

A Jewish synagogue, however, attracted his attention, and entering it, he claimed his right as a recognized teacher to speak, and there he presented the gospel, disputing with the adherents of Judaism, and with proselytes who were doubtless weary of the unsatisfactory character of idolatrous rites and ceremonies, and had sought out this place of instruction in the law of Moses.

In the market place also he addressed himself to individuals, and sometimes little groups would gather about him to whom he proclaimed the wondrous story of God's grace in Christ Jesus to a lost world. Little by little he drew the attention of the people, who were always interested in that which seemed new and strange. So we need not be surprised that at last certain philosophers of the Epicureans and the Stoics became interested in him and his teaching.

The Epicureans

were those who said that man's supreme good is found in trying to please himself, that there is no use denying one's self; make the best of life by getting all the pleasure out of it you can, for you are going to be dead a long time. We can hear the echo of this in the philosophy of so-called self-expression of our day.

The Stoics took the opposite view of life. They said: We are in the hands of a remorseless fate; we had nothing to say about coming into the world, and there is no telling what will happen when we leave it. Just grit your teeth, don't show the white feather, make up your mind that "what cannot be cured must be endured." Stoicism has come down through the ages as the synonym for patient endurance.

Some of these philosophers asked, "What will this babbler say?" To them he seemed to be setting forth new gods. New gods in Athens! They had searched the world to find all of them. They had shrines for the gods of Babylon, Phoenicia, Greece, Egypt, and Rome. They worshiped them all, and yet this man seemed to know something about some ones, because Paul preached "Jesus and the resurrection." They thought that Anastasis (resurrection) was another god. They had the god of peace, the god of victory, the god of justice, the god of love—all these different deified human attributes; and now they thought, "This man seems to have two new gods, one called Jesus and the other, Resurrection. We would like to hear more about them." And they took him up to Mars' Hill, or the Areopagus. This overlooked Athens, and was where the philosophers met for discussion. So they invited Paul to come up there and expound his new doctrines. Led by them, he wended his way to the meeting-place above, and at once began to proclaim the message that he had been yearning to give them for so long.

He took his text from an inscription he had seen on one of their altars, and said, as it were, "I see you are a very religious people. You seem to worship every god known to the Greeks and all other nations, and as I walked about I noticed an altar with the inscription,

'To the Unknown God!'"

(Just such an altar has been unearthed recently). It was evident that these Athenians feared lest they might be neglecting some god whose name had not been communicated to them, and so they set up the altar that had attracted Paul's attention.

What a splendid text it made! And so Paul said, "Whom therefore ye ignorantly worship, him declare I unto you." In other words, "I am here to tell you who the unknown God is." How can anyone make known the unknown? God has made Himself known in the person of His blessed Son, the Lord Jesus Christ. Paul was there, indeed, to present Jesus and the resurrection, and let me say that no man preaches the gospel unless he does preach Jesus and the resurrection.

There is no gospel for guilty sinners apart from Christ, for the gospel is God's message about His blessed Son. The gospel is not good advice to be obeyed; it is *good news to be believed*. And that good news concerns the Lord Jesus Christ who came from the glory that He had with the Father from all eternity down to the sorrow and anguish of the cross of Calvary where He bared His breast that the sword of divine justice might be sheathed in His heart. He took our place and endured what we deserved. But that alone would not be the gospel; there is something more needed. Paul preached

Jesus, And—

And What? "*And* the resurrection." Every sermon that he ever preached was an Easter sermon; every sermon that the early apostles preached was an Easter sermon, for wherever they went they preached that Christ *died* for our sins according to the Scriptures: and that He was *buried*, and that He *rose again* the third day according to the Scriptures. The essence of their message was that He "was delivered for our offenses, and was raised again for our justification" (Rom. 4:25).

So Paul preached Jesus and the resurrection, and we today proclaim the same, and we tell you in His Name, "That if thou shalt confess with thy mouth the Lord Jesus, and shalt believe in thine heart that God hath raised him from the dead, thou shalt be saved. For with the heart man believeth unto righteousness; and with the mouth confession is made unto salvation" (Rom. 10:9, 10).

The Creator and the Created

Notice how Paul prepared the ground for his message. First of all, they were reminded that the Creator must be greater than that which is created, and Paul directed their attention to the visible universe. It was very evident that the God who made all things could not be confined in one of their temples. He says, "God that made the world and all things therein, seeing that he is Lord of heaven and earth, dwelleth not in temples made with hands; neither is worshiped with men's hands, as though he needed any thing, seeing he giveth to all life, and breath, and all things" (Acts 17:24, 25). He is not the God of one nation, but of all nations, and we are really one people, for He "hath made of one blood all nations of men for to dwell on all the face of the earth, and hath determined the times before appointed, and the bounds of their habitation." He has put upon men the responsibility to know Him, for He is not far from any one of us.

There is no man anywhere who will dare say in the day of judgment, "I wanted to find God and could not," for

Closer is He than breathing,
Nearer than hands and feet.

He is so close that if men will feel after Him, will stretch up empty hands towards Him, they will find His great strong hands reaching down to lay hold of them. God will never permit it to be said that any man honestly sought the way of life and failed to find it, that any man really wanted to be saved, and cried to God unheard.

This answers a question that troubles a good many people. I am often asked,

"What About the Heathen"

that have never heard the gospel? Are they going to be damned because they have never heard?" No matter where a heathen man may be today, if he wants to know God and honestly reaches out after Him, God will make Himself responsible to give that man light enough to be saved, for He is not far from any one of us. God has commanded men "that they should seek the Lord, if haply they might feel after him, and find him" (Acts 17:27).

This is the only place in the New Testament where we get the word *feel*. I have often urged people to trust the Lord Jesus, and have told them how He died for them, bore their sins on the cross, and that if they will believe on Him, He has given His own Word that "whosoever believeth in him should not perish, but have everlasting life." And then they say, "Well, I do *believe*, but I don't *feel* any different." That has nothing to do with it. The word *feel* is not a Christian word at all. The only place it occurs in the New Testament is here where Paul is speaking of the heathen. But you have an open Bible; you do not need to feel after God. What you need to do is to *believe* the testimony that He has given, and then you will be saved. "Believe on the Lord Jesus Christ, and thou shalt be saved, and thy house" (Acts 16:31). This is the word of the living God given through His servants of old.

"Feel" and "Feel ing"

I said that the word *feel* is found only once in the New Testament, but the word *feeling* is found twice: once in Ephesians 4:19, where it speaks of certain Gentiles, and says, "Who being past feeling have given themselves over unto lasciviousness, to work all uncleanness with greediness;" and again in Hebrews 4:15, "For we have not an high priest which cannot be touched with the feeling of our infirmities." Apart from these three instances we do not find the words *feeling* or *feel* used in the New Testament. The moment you believe in the Lord Jesus, the moment you trust in Him you pass out of death into life, out of condemnation into justification before the throne of God.

In John 5:24, Jesus says, "Verily, verily, I say unto you, He that heareth my word, and believeth him that sent me, hath everlasting life, and shall not come into condemnation; but is passed from death unto life." Notice the

Five Divisions of John 5:24

1. *"He That Heareth My Word."* Face this; be honest with your own heart. Have you heard the Word of the Son of God? Have you heard Him speaking to you through this blessed Book?

2. *"And Believeth Him That Sent Me."* Do you in your heart believe that God sent the Lord Jesus Christ to be the sinner's Savior, to die for you on the cross, to rise from the dead for your justification?

3. *"Hath Everlasting Life."* When do you get it? When you die? No, you get it *now*, from the moment you hear the Word of the Son of God, and receive and confess Him as the One whom the Father sent into the world to be the sinner's Savior. The trouble today is that people are stumbling over its very simplicity.

I heard of a man who wanted to be saved, and he was told to do penance for sin by putting hard dried peas in his shoes and walking on them so many hours a day. This poor man did this and limped around the streets, trying to make atonement. It would have done him just as much good if he had boiled the peas first.

But people are willing to do all kinds of hard things. They are like Naaman who, when the prophet commanded, "Go and wash in Jordan seven times," said, "That is too easy a way." But he had a wise old servant who suggested, "If the prophet had bid thee do some *great* thing, wouldest thou not have done it?" Why, of course he would. "How much rather then, when he saith to thee, Wash, and be clean?" (2 Kings 5:10, 13). If you had to give a great deal of money, say a great many prayers, make long pilgrimages, do vast numbers of charitable deeds in order to get life eternal, how many of you would be willing to do these things? How much more when He saith to thee, *"Believe and live!"*

4. *"Shall Not Come Into Condemnation."* Think of it! The Roman Catholic Version reads, "Amen, amen, I say unto you, whoso hears my word and believes him that sent me, has eternal life and comes not into judgment, but is passed out of death into life." Is that not good news? Not a word about purgatory, not a word about confession to a priest, not a word about sacramental observances, not a word about penance; but here and now, the moment you put your trust in the Lord Jesus Christ, your sins are gone and you will never come into judgment, but you have everlasting life. It is all for you. That is the gospel which Paul preached. And notice the next point:

5. *"Is Passed From Death Unto Life."* It is settled, complete salvation, giving a new standing before God to the believing sinner. Observe the threefold link with resurrection.

1. Resurrection and Repentance

But what if men do not accept it? Then there is the judgment. He says that God has been very gracious with the heathen: "The times of this ignorance God winked at; but now commandeth all men everywhere to *repent*" (Acts 17:30). Repent means to change your mind completely, to have a new attitude. You had an idea that you could save yourself by your good works, but you change your mind and now admit that you cannot do a thing to save yourself, but that Christ must do it all. That is repentance—a change of attitude toward God. Instead of trying to do anything to save yourself, let the Lord Jesus do it all.

God "commandeth all men everywhere to repent: because he hath appointed a day, in the which he will judge the world in righteousness by that man whom he hath ordained." God is going to judge the world in righteousness, but your case can be settled out of court, and settled today, so that you need never think of coming into judgment. But if you reject Christ, some day you must give account before His judgment throne.

2. Resurrection and Assurance

"Whereof he hath given *assurance* unto all men, in that he hath raised him from the dead." The resurrection of the body of our Lord Jesus Christ is the ground of our assurance that we shall live again in our resurrected bodies. He says, "Because I live, ye shall live also." We are told that "as in Adam all die, even so in Christ shall all be made alive." This does not mean that all men will be saved, but that the bodies of all men will be raised from the dead. Thus God has given assurance to all men of a life after death in that He raised the body of Christ from the grave. In the second place He has given assurance unto all men that the sin question is settled in the death of Christ, by raising His body from the dead.

Here is an innocent man who has gone to prison for the crime of another. He knew the other man was guilty, but he knew, too, that in order to prove his own innocence he would have to expose his friend; and so he hears the sentence of the judge, sending him to prison for one year. What must be the feeling of the other man outside? He says, "I have sent that man there; I deserved to go, but he is there in my place." Perhaps he goes to see him and the man says, "I took your place voluntarily, and I am quite content; you let me endure it." The other roams the streets and says, "I wonder how long he will be content to remain there; I wonder how long before he tells the whole story." But by and by a year has passed, and walking down the street one day, he sees the one who went to prison for him. He rushes up and says, "What does this mean?"

"It means," is the reply, "that you have nothing to fear now. The sentence has all been endured."

So our blessed Lord bore on the Tree the sentence for us, and now we who were once guilty sinners are free. "Christ being raised from the dead dieth no more." The resurrection is the proof that the sin question has been settled, that God is satisfied. "He hath given assurance unto all men, in that he hath raised him from the dead."

3. Resurrection and Reckoning

In the third place we have assurance in the resurrection of Jesus Christ that some day all men are going to give account to Him. This will be when He sits upon the great white throne. Think of giving account of your sins to Him after all He has done to save you from them!

Notice the threefold response that Paul's message had that day. "When they heard of the resurrection of the dead, some mocked: and others said, we will hear thee again of this matter. . . . Howbeit certain men clave unto him, and believed" (Acts 17:32, 34). I wonder if there are not people manifesting these three different attitudes toward that message today! Some mock, some ridicule, some say, "Oh, we cannot believe this message about Jesus and the resurrection; we cannot accept it. We do not see how He could die for sinners and rise again, and how men can be saved through believing on Him." God pity you if you are turning this message down. Some day He will turn you down, for He says in His Word, "Because I have called, and ye refused; I have stretched out my hand, and no man regarded; but ye have set at nought all my counsel, and would none of my reproof: I also will laugh at your calamity; I will mock when your fear cometh" (Prov. 1:24-26). God grant that you may not at last be exposed to such a doom. Do not turn it down, do not go away with a cold, careless sneer and say, "It is nothing to me."

The second class said, "We will hear thee again of this matter." They are the procrastinators. You may not be mocking; possibly you would not sneer at the gospel message; you fully intend to be saved some day, but you are saying, "I will hear you again, I am not ready to close with Christ today. There is so much to occupy my heart and mind these days; some other time. Let me alone for the present. Sometime I will give attention to these things." Remember the old saying, "Procrastination is the thief of time." There is a Spanish proverb which says, "The road of by and by leads to the town of never." How many have taken that road, have said, "By and by, some other day." and have gone on and on, until at last they have reached the other world, hopelessly lost, and that forever!

The third class, "Howbeit certain men clave unto him, and believed." What a blessed testimony! God has recorded the names of two of them, one man and one woman, Dionysius and Damaris, who accepted the message proclaimed that day.

Men have an idea that what sinners need is more culture, more refinement; but if polite culture could have saved the world, Greece would have been saved long ago. But *Greece went all to pieces in spite of its culture.* It was the gospel of the grace of God that saved the ancient world from ruin. And it is the gospel of the Lord Jesus Christ that saves men today. I bring before you these two examples, Dionysius and Damaris, and I beg you to follow them as they followed Christ; believe the message, and go on rejoicing in Him, who was raised from the dead, never to die again. Hear what He says in Revelation 1:18: "I am he that liveth, and was dead; and, behold, I am alive for evermore."

Jesus Is Alive

George W. Truett (1867-1944) was perhaps the best-known Southern Baptist preacher of his day. He pastored the First Baptist Church of Dallas, Texas, from 1897 until his death, and saw it grow both in size and influence. Active in denominational ministry, Truett served as President of the Southern Baptist Convention and for five years was President of the Baptist World Alliance; but he was known primarily as a gifted preacher and evangelist. Nearly a dozen books of his sermons were published.

This sermon was taken from *The Salt of the Earth*, published in 1949 by the Broadman Press.

George W. Truett

6

JESUS IS ALIVE

Fear not. I am he that liveth, and was dead; and, behold, I am alive for evermore, Amen; and have the keys of hell and of death (Revelation 1:17, 18).

IN THE LAST book of the Bible, in its first chapter is found our text: "Fear not. I am he that liveth and was dead; and, behold, I am alive for evermore, Amen; and have the keys of hell and death."

This was the word of good cheer from Jesus to the frightened, disheartened servant, John, on the isle of Patmos. The habit of good cheer is a blessed habit, and everyone of us should see to it that such habit is regnant in our lives. The Bible magnifies that habit. It tells us: "A merry heart doeth good like a medicine" (Prov. 17:22). And we find that sunny precept shining out from Paul's statements in the midst of his greatest tribulations: "Rejoice evermore." The Bible every where magnifies this wonderful habit of good cheer, and everyone of us should see to it that it is uppermost in our lives.

Our habits are the things which have and hold us, and very largely make or mar our lives. The habit of good cheer is an asset of priceless worth. One's battles are the more successfully fought if they be fought with the spirit of good cheer. One's sicknesses are the more quickly overcome if they are faced with the spirit of good cheer. One's burdens, however weighty they may be, are the more easily borne if they are borne in the spirit of good cheer. Nor is that all. This matter of being sunshiny, of being men and women of the cheerful, hopeful spirit, affects all around us as well as ourselves. As we sing or do not sing, we affect the people about us, for we radiate influence from ourselves to bless everybody or hurt everybody, to give them weights or to give them wings.

> A singer sang a song of tears,
> And the great world listened and wept;
> For he sang of the sorrows of fleeting years,
> And hopes which the dead past kept,
> And souls who in anguish their burden bore,
> Looked down and went weeping as never before.
>
> A singer sang a song of cheer,
> And the great world listened and smiled,
> For he sang of the love of a Father dear,
> And the trust of a little child.
> And souls who before had forgotten to pray,
> Looked up and went singing along the way.

It is the business of Jesus and His gospel, His mission and His message, to deliver us from slavish fear. John, on the isle of Patmos, banished there because of his fealty to Jesus and his testimony for Jesus, was all down in spirit and there was given him revelation after revelation from the glory world, and John was overcome by the glory of the revelations. And he fell down as one dead in his fright, the Scripture says, and Jesus spoke to him the blessed words of our text: "Fear not. I am he that liveth and was dead; and, behold, I am alive for evermore, Amen; and have the keys of hell and death." Jesus had the keys of the invisible world. He had conquered death and the grave.

These words are full of meaning for us. We do well to ponder them this Lord's day evening. I have said that it is the business of Jesus, the mission of Jesus, the message of Jesus, to deliver us from fear, servile, enervating, undoing fear; and we, in turn, are to walk in His steps and to help people about us constantly.

Great meanings are in this simple statement that Jesus made to John. Life and death and the eternal hereafter, all are here in this statement made by Jesus. Let us look at these meanings.

Christ Delivers Us From the Timorous Fear of Life

First of all, Jesus would deliver us from the slavish fear of life. Is there fear in life? Is such fear real? Do people ever get afraid? Ah me! How many times people start back and shrink away and feel affrighted by life! That fear is real. For we are so keenly conscious, at times, of our absolute dependence upon God.

And then we are conscious of our dependence upon one another. Men sometimes use that big word, "independent." Independent of what? Of whom? Everyone of us is under the necessity of praying: "Give us this day our daily bread." The richest man in the world needs to pray that, as well as the poorest. He has his stocks and bonds, his vast material treasures and his gold. But he cannot live on them. He must live from hand to mouth, each day. Every human being, the strongest and the wealthiest, is utterly dependent upon God. And then we are dependent upon one another. How far would we get without the cooperation of others? How far would we get but for our contacts and our sympathies and our cooperations with humanity all about us? When we realize our absolute dependence upon God, and upon our fellow humans, we are apt to be filled with fear because of our own inadequacy to grapple with life.

And then added to that we have life about us with its mysteries and they are on every side, and they confront us every time we open the windows of our minds and give ourselves to thought. There is the mystery of God, the immeasurable, infinite, omniscient, eternal, omnipresent God. There is the mystery of sin in the world about us. Oh, its reigning power and its bedarkening work! There is the mystery of it. And there is the mystery of Providence everywhere. In a time like this, when the world is in its Gethsemane, when it looks as if it were going to be stretched upon a cross before all is over, how our hearts start back with amazement and with fear, and we cry out for light. We cry out as a child in the dark for some assuring voice.

And then we go on and face life's responsibilities. How we start back! You know what that means. Life's responsibilities! Here is this or that or the other upon me. How shall I get through with these things? Here are these relationships which I cannot ignore. How shall I get through with them? Shall I make good? Can I make good?

Will I measure up to my duty? Will I measure up to my responsibility? One little earthly life have I to live. Will I make good now with this life? Questions like these ever come to serious men and women. And then we face our tasks, our trusts, and how they do depress us! How they weigh upon us, when we seriously lay them to heart!

Do you remember how it was when you first left home? I remember as vividly as though it were yesterday, when I went away the first time to the outside world, to meet it for myself. I remember the good-bye with the loved ones at home, and what they each said to me as I went away to the call and the tasks of the untried world. Frankly, I confess to you that during those first few miles of the road leading from my home I felt much more like crying than singing. When I looked back from a hill and saw my home nestling among the great trees I felt a lump in my throat and a tremor in my heart.

For the first time, I was going out to the great world to meet it all alone, and my heart sank within me. I asked: "How shall I face the trust that has been thrust upon me? How shall I face the task to which I have been called? How shall I measure up to the position to which I go? Shall I make good? Can I make good?" Oh, the fears that shoot through us like so many arrows in an hour like that! And these hours of responsibility, of change, of new duties, of unexpected tasks, of weighty responsibilities, of great calls, come to us all along in life, and the tendency is with us many times to start back all frightened.

Jesus comes to us in such hours, saying: "Fear not to live. I am alive and I am with you—nearer to you than hands or feet, nearer to you than breathing, nearer to you than Mother ever was, nearer to you than the closest earthly friend or dearest earthly form. I am with you. I am with you always. I am with you whatever comes." So, dear friend, whatever your task, your trust, your duty, your responsibility, fear not! Go to that task or that post without hesitation. Divine power and reinforcement are available for you.

That changes it all. Why should a man be nerveless and heartsick and afraid, with Christ Jesus at his side every day and everywhere? That is what He says: "Fear not to live. I am alive, and I will hear your call, and I will be by your side, and I will reinforce you for every task."

Fear not to live because of the sorrows that shall come upon you, as come they will, sooner or later. The Spanish proverb has in it truth for us all when it says: "There is no home that sooner or later will not have its hush." The proverb carries its own meaning. There will be shadows, there will be clouds, the windows will be darkened. The hush comes sooner or later to every home. Jesus comes to us saying: "Fear not. When that day comes with its hush, its clouds, its shadows and its tears, I will be right there, closer than any earthly friend. You can turn to me for rest unto your soul. You can utterly trust me, for I will never fail you. Fear not to live."

Christ Delivers Us From the Slavish Fear of Death

Jesus has another great word of comfort and assurance for us. He would deliver us from the slavish fear of death. Fear not to die. The thought of death fills many with a nameless fear. It is a borne from which no traveler has returned to tell us about it. That passage down through the valley of the shadow is an experience from which we start back with quaking and shuddering and with a sigh. Now Jesus comes to deliver us from the slavish fear of dying. Some people are all their lifetime in bondage through fear of death. I think this moment of a remarkably clever woman, whom I knew for years and years, and every time I had a serious conversation with her through these years, she said to me: "The thought of death and the presence of death are something terrifying to me. I would never go into the death chamber," she said, "if I could avoid it. I would never go to a funeral if conditions, if duty, would at all allow me to absent myself." All her lifetime she was in bondage through fear of death. Jesus would not have it so, because death is just a change. That is all; just a change, and a change for the friend of God immediately and infinitely better. Fear not to die. But, since no one has ever come back to tell us about it, we are afraid.

Spiritualism is a vain effort to satisfy that great longing in the human heart. There is a deep desire to speak to our loved ones who have gone. Personally, I think that Spiritualism is a snare and a delusion. Dead people do not talk to living people at all. That is not God's plan. And yet, I can well understand how people yearn for some word from their loved ones who have died. One of the many indictments that I would bring against this doctrine of Spiritualism is that what these people are alleged to say to the living, and the revelations that they purpose to give, is so often mere drivel.

Has anybody come back to tell us? One has come. Jesus said: "I have come back. I was dead but am alive forevermore. I went down into the valley of the shadow. I met death. I conquered death. I have come back to tell you that you need not be afraid." I have been into the chamber of death. I have explored its every portal. I have come back with the keys of death swinging at my girdle. I am victor over death. I hold the keys. Now you need not be afraid." That is the meaning of what He said to John on Patmos. Therefore I do not need to consult Spiritualism. I have something a thousand times surer than all that. I have the sure word of Christ who said: "I was dead, and behold, I am alive for evermore."

They saw Him put to death and they saw Him laid in Joseph's new tomb, and they saw Him on that third day, when he came out of that grave, and they saw Him during the forty days following. He revealed Himself to small companies, and to large companies, and the one great fact on this Sunday night is that Jesus, crucified on Golgotha, and laid in Joseph's new tomb, came out of the grave, and is victor over death, alive now forevermore.

Fear not to die. The Conqueror of death went down into death and came back with the keys of death swinging at His girdle, my Savior, my Lord! Fear not to die. Fear not when your time comes. Worry not about it. Have no gloomy forebodings. Conjure up to yourself no dark and dismal hours. Oh, fear not to die. Go right on. Stand at your post. Sing, though the shadows thicken about you. Jesus says: "I will go down through the valley of the shadow with you and I will turn the very shadow of death into morning for you."

I saw one of our fine men of this congregation die awhile back. In the early morning, as the grey of the dawn began to show in the east, he called, oh so tenderly, to the wife of his heart, called her by name, and said: "It is just as dark, my dear, as it can be, I cannot see at all. Evidently this is the last. I wish that you would get just as close to me as you can. Hold my hand." And she did, of course, as he begged her to do. Presently all that was changed, and calling her by an endearing name, he said: "Dear, you need not be troubled anymore. Jesus has come and He has my hand, and I am in His great arms, and I know He is here." And then he said to her and to the rest of us in the room: "Can you see Him? Did anybody ever see such a face as that?" And then he said: "Can you hear the music? Oh, the rapture of these heavenly harmonies! Can you hear them?" As he went down into the valley of the shadow of death he said: "The Lord is my Shepherd." It was the very vestibule of heaven. Fear not to die!

You heard some of us tell about that Scotch Presbyterian preacher, John McNeil, one of the world's greatest preachers, who preached on the Pacific coast years ago, when some of us were there on the same platform, speaking with him. He gave six addresses on the Twenty-third Psalm, marvelous, incomparable Psalm, and he gave one on this: "Yea, though I walk through the valley of the shadow of death, I will fear no evil; for Thou art with me, Thy rod and Thy staff, they comfort me." He illustrated it at last by letting us see a glimpse of his boyhood life in Scotland. He toiled in a certain community from Monday morning until Saturday night, and then he tramped down the country road, when the work was done, to his own home, miles away, so that he could be with his loved ones at home on Sunday, just as much as possible. He said that some Saturday nights his tasks kept him late, and he always went down that road homeward in the late night time afraid, because the country was infested with robbers, and serious troubles came because of the robbers.

One Saturday night he was later than ever, practically

until midnight getting through his tasks, which he always finished before he went home. He said that the night was so dark he could not see his hand before his face, as he groped his homeward way. Along that road, that fearful, black, midnight hour, he went toward home, wondering if robbers would come out to halt him and harm him. As he trudged along, he heard footsteps coming. He stopped and they stopped. When he started again, so did those approaching footsteps. Again he stopped and they stopped. Then out from that blackness of the midnight there came a voice: "Is that you Johnny?" It was his father's voice. "I suppose I got home," he said. "I reckon I would not be here if I had not. But what did I care for all those miles of travel? What did I care for the darkness? What did I care for the late hours? What did I care for the robbers? My father had come after me, my friend, my protector, my champion, my great defender." He was more than enough for all the robbers of the dark night.

John McNeil said, "The rest of the way I walked through the valley of the shadow of utter darkness that midnight, but without fear. My father was with me." And then he turned in his own quaint Scotch way and told us: "Oh, when the time comes, and you go down through the valley of the shadow of death, and the darkness shall settle about you, and the earthly forms and faces shall all recede, and everything human and earthly shall slip away, be not afraid. For Jesus says: 'I am alive and I will hold thee, and I will guide thee, and I will keep thee, because I have conquered death for all my friends'."

Christ Delivers Us From the Morbid Fear of What Follows Death

There is one more word. Jesus will not only deliver us from a timorous fear of life, and deliver us from a slavish fear of death, but Jesus will deliver us from a morbid fear of what is coming after death. "Fear not to live for I am alive. Fear not to die for I have died. I have conquered death, and I am alive forevermore. Fear not what is coming after death, because I hold in my hand the keys." Keys indicate authority. Keys indicate control. "I have in my hands," said Jesus, "the keys to all the invisible world. Fear not, my friend, what is coming after death."

Belief in God carries with it belief in immortality. If a man believes deeply and truly in God, he also believes in immortality. "If a man die shall he live again?" Do you believe in a supreme Being? Then you believe in immortality. Even the heathen nations, with their little, faint, tallow candles of spiritual light, believe in immortality, in a way. The Chinese groping in darkness, believe in a form of immortality. I am glad they do, so that when missionaries go with their larger light of revealed religion to those groping in darkness, they have some spiritual foundation to build on. Belief in immortality goes hand in hand with belief in God.

Belief in a day of judgment is an essential corollary to a belief in immortality. Reason demands a day of judgment. There are so many irregularities, so many tangled skeins, so many inequalities. There is unrighteousness flourishing and reigning and for a season rampant and seemingly triumphant. There must be a day of reckoning, a court of assize, a tribunal where all shall be interpreted and judged and explained. Our reason calls for it. And then when we open the Holy Scriptures, the infallible rule of faith and practice for humanity, God's own divinely given revelation for the guidance of humanity, when we open the Scriptures, clear are they as the sunlight, that there is a Judgment day. We must all appear before the judgment seat of Christ. We must every one give account of himself to God.

Jesus said: "If you will cling to me; if you will accept me as your Savior, Guide and Master of your life, you need not be afraid even of that tribunal known as the final Judgment. You need not be afraid to live, if you are my friend, nor afraid to die, no matter where nor how nor when. If you are my friend, you need not be afraid of anything beyond death, through all the ages eternal. Where I am there ye shall be also."

Oh, where Jesus is there is where I want to be. Where He goes, that is where I want to go. It will be heaven anywhere to be with Jesus. "I go to prepare a place for you, and if I go and prepare a place for you, I will come again, and receive you unto myself, that where I am, there ye may be also" (John 14:2, 3). How glorious!

Christ is the road for life, for death, for the eternal future. What if you miss that road? What if you do not cling to Christ? If you turn away from the light He gives, pray what light will you follow? Be for Christ. Oh, be for Christ! If you ask me what is my supreme hope, I will point you to Christ.

> Other refuge have I none,
> Hangs my helpless soul on Thee.

Nor do I wish any other refuge. "I have found Him whom my soul loveth," Jesus who died on the Cross, and was buried in the tomb, and who came there from victor over death and sin and the grave. My hope, my Righteousness, my Redeemer, my Lord, my God, I trust Him, I cling to Him, and He alone is my hope forever. Is He yours? I pause before we pray, to ask every soul in this place whose trust is in Christ as your personal Savior, every man and woman who can say, "He is," lift your hand, please. That is a great sight. I thank you.

Every Sunday morning and night here, we ask those present who are not Christians, to accept Christ as Savior and Lord, and to go with us in His service. So, I pause to ask, is there somebody in all this press tonight whose hand was not lifted a moment ago, because you have not accepted the offered salvation of Christ; you have not said "Yes" to His call; you have not surrendered your will and your life to His guidance?

Is there somebody who says: "I did not lift my hand because I have not made that great surrender"? Would you like for us to offer a prayer for you before we go, that it may be well with you, that you may be saved, that your soul, your life, your all may be bound up with Christ, according to His will? Lift high your hand and we will pray that you will give yourself unreservedly and whole heartedly into Christ's keeping tonight. Lift them now!

Yes, yes, yes, I see your uplifted hands here, there and yonder throughout this congregation and I am sure that Christ sees them also. We who trust Him and seek to follow Him will all pray for you now that you be enabled to yield your hearts and wills unto Him as Savior and Lord, even now.

Easter Triumph

John Daniel Jones (1865-1942), "Jones of
Bournemouth," was one of England's best-known preachers
and denominational leaders. Ordained in 1889, Jones
pastored in Lincoln and then became a New Testament
lecturer in the Nottingham Theological Institute. In 1898
he went to Richmond Hill Congregational Church,
Bournemouth, where he ministered with distinction for
40 years. He published many books of sermons, but
perhaps his best work is his *Commentary on Mark*.

"Easter Triumph" is from *The Gospel of Grace* (Baker
Book House, reprinted 1976). It is interesting to compare
this message with the one on the same text by George W.
Truett.

John Daniel Jones

7

EASTER TRIUMPH

And I was dead, and behold, I am alive for evermore, and I have the keys of death and of Hades (Revelation 1:18).

THUS DOES THAT radiant Person whom John saw on the Lord's day in the Isle of Patmos, whose head and whose hair were white as white wool, white as snow, whose eyes were as a flame of fire, and His feet like unto burnished brass, and His voice like the voice of many waters, set forth, shall I say, the salient points in His own history. The central and all-important facts of our Lord's history, according to my text, are these two: He *became dead—He is alive.* We are grateful for the other deeds He did when upon earth, for the cleansing He gave to the leper, and the hearing He gave to the deaf, and for the sight He gave to the blind, and for the speech He gave to the dumb, for the comfort He gave to the sad, and the hope He gave to the hopeless. But those are not the critical and all-important acts of our Lord's life. It is conceivable that there might have been a Christian church if He had never healed the sick, if there had been no story of Bartimaeus, or of the sick of the palsy, or of the man born blind, to tell. But there never would have been a church at all without a Cross and a Resurrection. Here are the two supreme facts of the Christian religion, the foundation stone of the Christian faith—*He became dead—He is alive.* And these two facts are the facts which Easter celebrates. The facts of Easter and the joy of Easter are all in my text. For notice what we have in it. (1) We have death—"I became dead." (2) We have life—"Behold I am alive for evermore." (3) We have the supremacy of life over death—"I have the keys of death and of Hades." It is about the facts of Easter and the joy of Easter that I want briefly to speak.

85

The Death of Christ

First, then, we have here the fact of the *death of Christ*.
"I was dead." It is in vain that anyone tries to thrust the
death of Christ from its central place in the Christian
gospel. The Cross is the beating and throbbing heart of
the faith. From His baptism to the end of His life Christ
looked forward to the Cross as the goal of all His endeavors,
the supreme act He had to accomplish, the work His Father
had given Him to do. And, looking back upon His earthly
life, it is still His dying that stands forth as His greatest
deed. It towers above every other act of His life as Mont
Blanc does among the Alps. It was no Pauline invention,
this emphasis upon the Cross. Our Lord laid the emphasis
in the same place. "Fear not," He said to John, "I am the
First and the Last and the Living One, and I *became dead*."
No single act of His life does our Lord mention. He passes
over His matchless parables and wondrous words without
a reference; He passes over His acts of grace and power
without a single hint of them, for the supreme act of His
life was the act in which it ended. "I am the First and the
Last and the Living One, and I *became dead*."

The death of Christ differed from the death of every
other person in the world. Other men *suffer* death; Christ,
shall I say, *achieved* it. To other men death comes to
frustrate work. Christ's death consummated, crowned, and
completed His work. It was on the Cross and from the
Cross Christ uttered that triumphant cry, "It is finished!"
The death of Christ was His greatest work, His supreme
act, His most glorious achievement! Now, about the death
of Christ, my text practically says two things.

It insists upon the reality of His death. "I became *dead*,"
says our risen and glorified Lord. There were those in the
early centuries who denied the reality of the death of
Christ, by asserting that the Christ descended upon Jesus
at His baptism and left Him again at His crucifixion. It
was the mere human shell, they said, that was crucified.
The Christ, the Divine Person, experienced nothing of the
shame and pain of the Cross.

There are those again in more recent times who assert
that our Lord did not die at all, that He only swooned or

fainted upon the Cross. Now this statement of my text cuts right athwart both those theories. It repudiates and contradicts them both. Was it the mere human shell from which the Christ had already escaped that suffered on the Cross? That is not what I read. "I am the First and the Last and the Living One, and I became dead." It might have been written specially to refute that gnostic heresy which made the Cross a mere show. "I, the First and the Last and the Living One, *I* became dead." It was not a mere simulacrum, a sort of phantom Jesus, who hung upon the Cross. It was the Eternal Son of God who there tasted death for every man! And equally does it repudiate the modern notion that Christ only swooned. "I became a dead man." That ugly, grim, forbidding word "dead" could have been applied to Jesus after that final cry upon the Cross. There was no sham or make-believe about what happened on Calvary. "I became dead." Indeed, I feel half inclined to say that our Lord's death was the only *real death* the world has ever known. At any rate, this is true—He tasted the *full bitterness of death* as no one ever did before and no one has ever done since.

What makes the end *death*? Sin. "The wages of sin is *death*." Had there been no sin—I do not say men's lives would never come to an end, but I do say that end would not have been *death*. Now Jesus did no sin Himself, but He made our sin His own. He who knew no sin became sin for us. He took upon His own head and heart all the shame and pain and guilt of our sin. And it was that sin of ours that made Christ's death the most real and awful death the world has ever known. For remember this: the more pure and holy the soul the more sensitive it is to the shame of sin. The more delicately and highly developed the physical organism, the more liable it is to physical suffering. Here in the midst of our highly-developed English civilization we are subject to an exquisiteness of pain of which the Red Indian or the African savage, with his rougher and harder nature, seems quite incapable. And it is exactly so too in the realms of the spirit. The purer the soul the sharper the pain it may feel. The ordinary man by his very sinfulness has bred in his soul a certain callousness to the pain of sin. But Jesus, with His absolutely pure and holy soul, felt it as no one else could feel it. When He took upon Him the sin of man He had to bear and receive the wages of it, and that wages was death. "The sting of death is sin," says St. Paul. The sting of Christ's death was sin—our sin which He made His own. And it stung Him as it could sting no one else, with the result that Christ's death was the most real and awful death the world has ever known. In fact, I will be bold enough to say that in its fullest and deepest sense, in the sense of exhausting all that death means in the shape of horror and darkness, the holy Jesus was the only one who really *died*. This was a real death—"I became dead."

We can comfort ourselves with the thought that whatever death is, Jesus knows it. That wherever death may lead men to, Jesus has explored the way! And this is what makes Him a perfect Friend and Helper. Had He never stooped to the grave He would have been unable to help us in the supreme experiences of life! He would have left us helpless just where we need help most. But He did not shrink even from death. He went down even into the grave. He became dead! And by that fact He is able to help and succor this race of dying men.

The phrasing of my text in the second place emphasizes and insists upon the *voluntariness of the death of Christ*. John uses here quite a remarkable phrase. Unfortunately both the Authorized Version and the Revised Version fail to reproduce it in the text, though the Revised Version does insert it in the margin. "And I was dead," so the text reads. But that is not what the First and the Last said to John. What He said was, "I *became* dead." And it is the absolute freedom and voluntariness of the death of Christ the special form of the phrase is meant to emphasize. I said a moment ago that Christ died really. He passed through that same solemn experience through which we shall all have to pass. But in one critical respect Christ's death differs from the death of every one else. He *became* dead. You say, "He died," of every one else. But of Jesus Christ "He *became* dead." Other people die because they cannot help it. But Jesus *willed* to die. He laid down His life. He *gave up the ghost.* He *became* dead. "No man taketh my life from Me, but I lay it down of Myself, I have power to lay it down and I have power to take it again" (John 10:18). The Cross in its reality and willingness—a reality and willingness which are necessary if it is to be a sacrifice—is the fact which the first phrase of my text sets forth.

The Resurrection of Christ

And secondly you have here in my text, *the resurrection of Christ.* "I became dead, and *behold I am alive.*" I do not know that we should celebrate Easter with joy and song if John's message had finished with that first statement, "I became dead." Even though the death of Christ were entirely voluntary, I do not know that the thought of it would bring us any comfort if the grave were the end of it all. It would remain perhaps the most beautiful and pathetic of martyrdoms, but beautiful and pathetic though it might be, it would be a cause of sorrow and despair, rather than of hope and triumph. The Christian church celebrates our Lord's death as His triumph and regards His Cross as His Royal Throne. We sing—

> In the Cross of Christ I glory,
> Towering o'er the wrecks of time.

We cheer our souls with the belief that the Cross is the pledge and instrument of victory. We see it leading us on in our conflicts and struggles, with Constantine's legend still written around it, *Tovtw vika,* "By this conquer."

But if the Cross was the very end, it is no cause for gladness and glorying. If the Cross was the very end, it stands for defeat, and disaster, and utter overthrow. If the Cross was the very end, then no one in the world's history has ever escaped the power of death, but death is this world's universal lord. If the Cross was the very end, then there has been no sacrifice for sin, and you and I shall each of us have to bear our terrible burden—"the wages of sin is death." If the Cross was the very end, then is our preaching vain, and your faith also vain, and the belief of the church throughout the centuries vain, and the sufferings of confessors and martyrs vain. We are yet in our sins! If it be true, as Matthew Arnold puts it, in that familiar verse of his:

Now He is dead! Far hence He lies,
In the lone Syrian town,
And on His grave, with shining eyes,
The Syrian stars look down,

then I would not summon you to glory in the Cross. I would summon you to imitate those maidens of the Lycus who commemorated the death of Adonis—the ruthless destruction of their noblest and best—with lamentation and woe. I would summon you to come and weep and wail at the cross as at the grave of our every hope.

But thank God the Cross is not the end. "Fear not," said the First and the Last to John, "I became dead, and behold I am alive." Alive! Death was not able to hold Jesus Christ! Reinforced as death was by the great stone, and the seal, and the soldiers, death was not able to hold Jesus Christ. On the third day the grave was found empty, and certain women came to the disciples reporting they had seen a vision of angels, who said that He was alive! *Alive!* That is the glorious fact that Easter commemorates. It sheds its radiance back upon Good Friday, and changes what would otherwise have been a martyrdom into an atoning sacrifice, so that at the Cross men are loosed from their sins; it changes the bitter tree into a royal seat, so that we march into our every battle "with the Cross of Jesus going on before." It sheds its radiance forward, so that we walk all our days in the light of it, for Jesus Christ is *alive. Alive!* Oh that, as in Dr. Dale's case we might realize that blessed fact! Alive! Jesus Christ alive! Just as much and just as truly alive as you and I.

Ah, but some one objects, Jesus is not the only one who came back from death. There have been others who were dead and became alive. And you remind me of the old Scripture stories of the Shunammite's little son and Jairus's daughter and the widow's son at Nain, and most marvelous of all, of Lazarus, who had been in the grave four days. But they became alive only to die again. They did not escape death, they only balked him of his prey for a few short years. The Shunammite's son, Jairus's daughter, the widow's son at Nain, Lazarus himself— they have gone the way of all flesh. Death got them all at the last. May it not have been so with Jesus Christ? No, it was not so with Jesus Christ. He did not come to life for a time merely. It was not a temporary escape from the power of death that He accomplished. List, "Fear not, I am the First and the Last and the Living One. And I became dead, and behold I am *alive for evermore!*" Forevermore! "Christ," says St. Paul, "being raised from the dead, dieth no more, death hath no more dominion over Him." He went down to the grave and there He struggled and fought with death and there He won His victory over death. It was a final victory, a conclusive victory. Death can never again reassert its power. Christ dieth no more. Death hath no more dominion over Him! "Behold, I am alive for evermore!"

And that is one reason why we rejoice at Easter. *Christ is alive and He will be alive forever*! He has been alive and with His people all down the centuries! He is alive and with His people today; He will be alive and with His people to the end. Jesus Christ alive! He was in our yesterdays; He is in our todays; and thank God He will be in our tomorrows. "With *Thee* I will go to prison and to death," said one of the disciples. With Jesus at his side he felt equal to any sacrifice and suffering. With Jesus at our side we too feel we can do anything and bear anything and face anything. With Jesus at our side we feel we shall not fear, though the earth be removed and though the mountains be carried into the midst of the sea. With Jesus at our side we feel we can meet trouble and fight temptation and endure loss. Holding Jesus's hand we feel we dare even venture without trembling into the valley of the shadow of death. "With Thee" we will go anywhere, everywhere. Well, is there any chance of losing Him? Can anything, can death snatch Him from our sides? No, never! "Lo, I am with you always, even to the end of the world." "I am the First and the Last and the Living One, and I became dead, and behold I *am alive* for evermore."

Christ's Supremacy Over Death

But there is more in my text than the death and resurrection of Christ. There is in my text also the assertion of our Lord's *supremacy over death*. "I have the keys of death and Hades." And this brings me to what is, perhaps, after all, the chief element of our Easter joy, namely, this, that when our Lord rose from the dead, He not only won escape for Himself, but He won escape and deliverance *for us*. "The Lord is risen" is the salutation of Easter morning. But I can imagine a man saying, "Even if it be true, what is that to me?" Well, it is *everything!* For when Jesus rose, it did not mean that He and He alone of all earth's millions had escaped death's power. It meant that He had conquered death, and that He had taken death captive; that He had clean abolished death; death has no more dominion over us. And that is the truth embodied in the last clause of my text.

"I became dead, and behold I am alive for evermore." There is comfort and solace in that statement, for it gives us amid the trials and conflicts of life a Present Christ, an Almighty Friend. And yet, if it finished there, we should feel that it had not banished every fear and dread. For it would leave the cold shadow of death still lying across our lives—a shadow that makes chill our very brightest day. But, thank God, it does not end there. "I was dead, and behold I am alive for evermore, and I *have the keys of death and of Hades!*" "I have the keys of death and of Hades." And that word "key" suggests to me two ideas.

First of all, C*hrist has told us death's secret*. He has shown us what death is. We talk, do we not, about possessing a *key* to a riddle. Well, Death is the greatest riddle that ever confronted and perplexed mankind. But Jesus Christ has, and indeed is, "the key" to it. One of the most profound and suggestive legends of ancient Greece was the legend of the Sphinx. The Sphinx, according to the old story, was a monstrous creature, half human, half animal, who had a riddle to propound to any travelers who passed her way. What exactly the riddle was does not matter to us just now. All that concerns us is that here was a creature propounding her riddle to men and exacting their lives as forfeit if they failed to answer it. Traveler after traveler, the legend says, tried and failed and perished. But at last there came one who discovered the answer, and the Sphinx, her secret discovered, destroyed herself. Whenever I think of that Greek legend I feel that from first to last it is nothing but a parable of death. Death is the Sphinx. Ever since the world began death has been in it propounding to mankind this tremendous riddle, "If a man die, shall he live again?", challenging them to discover her own secret, saying to them, "Explain me or pay the forfeit in a life passed in fear and bondage." And generation after generation tried to discover the secret and explain the riddle. The greatest sages and philosophers and teachers tried and failed. The psalmists and prophets of the Old Testament tried and failed. Death remained the terrible and inscrutable Sphinx.

But there came One at last who "became dead" and went down into the grave, and on the morning of the third day came out of it again. And now He says to the world, "*I have the key.*" Death is a secret no longer, an inscrutable mystery no longer, a terrifying darkness no longer. Christ knows what death is; He knows what lies on the other side of death. Millions have passed *through* the gates of death. But He, and He alone, has come back! "I have the key," He says to you and me. What, then, is death? Is it the pit, as the psalmist seems to imply? Is it the final end and extinction of life? No, says Jesus, it is but a brief passage-way into broader and ampler life. The last look on this world is "the first on God." Death has been robbed of its mystery, and because robbed of its mystery, robbed also of its terror. We do not need the investigations of a society of psychical research. It is Jesus Christ who has "the key." He brought "life and immortality to light."

And the word "key" suggests more than *secret*. It suggests also the idea of *power* and *authority*. The one who possesses "the keys" is the one vested with authority and rule. Well, our Lord has the keys of death and Hades. He has not only told us the secret of death, He has absolute mastery over death. He has subdued and taken captive and vanquished death. Do you remember that marvelous passage in the Hebrews which declare and enforces this truth? "Since, them," writes the author of that deep and wonderful letter, "the children are sharers in flesh and blood, He also Himself in like manner partook of the same, that through death He might bring to nought him that had the power of death, that is the devil, and might deliver all them who, through fear of death, were all their lifetime subject to bondage" (Heb. 2:14,15).

Till Christ's resurrection day the hour of death was the hour and power of darkness. But ever since He came forth from the grave He has stripped death of its power, and delivered all those who, through fear of death, were all their lifetime in bondage. The grave, we know, is no longer a prison-house of which death holds the key. Christ is Lord of death. Christ is King of that invisible world into which men pass. *I have the keys of death and Hades.*" And to know that the grave and all that lies beyond, form part of Christ's dominion is to lose one's fear of death. It is not some deadly foe of ours that is waiting for us when we enter the valley of the shadow. It is our gracious and loving Lord who is waiting for us. We have but to realize that, and death will cease to appear terrible and forbidding to us. We shall lay hands on death and say with Paul, "death is ours." We shall be able to say with that great apostle, "to die is gain."

Do you remember Hugh Mackail's final words on the scaffold? "Now I leave off to speak any more to creatures and turn my speech to Thee, O Lord. Now I begin my fellowship with God, which shall never be broken off. Farewell, father and mother, friends and relations! Farewell, meat and drink! Farewell, sun, moon and stars! Welcome God and Father! Welcome sweet Lord Jesus, the Mediator of the New Covenant! Welcome blessed Spirit of Grace! Welcome glory! Welcome eternal life! Welcome death!" That is splendid and magnificent triumph. That brave confessor and martyr knew that death had no more dominion over him, that in the darkness and shadow Jesus Christ was waiting for him.

That same happy and triumphant confidence may be

ours. Stevenson in his essays insists upon "being vital," as he calls it. Whatever else you are, he says, "be vital." He is encouraging and seeking to foster a brave and cheerful optimism. Do not trouble about death, says Stevenson, make the best of life. Now there is truth in that, and wisdom in it; and in all literature there is nothing I know of more touching than the zest with which Stevenson determined to live, though in his sickly body he carried all his days the sentence of death in himself. But after all, it is a poor business trying to ignore death.

"Being vital" is all very well, but to live as if life were to go on as it does now is the most senseless folly. But indeed death will not be ignored. We may whistle to keep our courage up; we may pretend there is no such thing as death; but there will be an end to our pretense some day, and we shall have to look death straight in the face. Stevenson himself confesses that his advice to "be vital" does not work. "With the best will," he writes in his touching preface to his *Virginibus Puerisque*, "no man can be twenty-five for ever," and he confesses that "the shadows of the prison-house" have closed upon him. But there need be no "shadows of the prison-house" creeping over our life. Our history may be that of the light which shineth more and more unto the perfect day. We may contemplate the end and say with the great Marquis of Argyle, "I am not afraid to be surprised with fear."

And it is Easter morning that brings us to that serene and happy confidence—for here to us on the Lord's Day, as to John in Patmos of old, the First and the Last and the Living One appears and says, "I became dead, and behold I am alive for evermore, and I have the keys of death and hell."

Horizoned by Resurrection

George Campbell Morgan (1863-1945) was the son of a British Baptist preacher and preached his first sermon when he was 13 years old. He had no formal training for the ministry, but his tireless devotion to the study of the Bible helped him to become one of the leading Bible teachers of his day. Rejected by the Methodists, he was ordained into the Congregational ministry. He was associated with Dwight L. Moody in the Northfield Bible conferences and as an itinerant Bible teacher. He is best known as the pastor of Westminster Chapel, London (1904-17 and 1933-45). During his second term there, he had Dr. D. Martyn Lloyd-Jones as his associate.

He published more than 60 books and booklets, and his sermons are found in *The Westminster Pulpit* (Pickering and Inglis Ltd., London). This sermon is from Volume 4.

George Campbell Morgan

8

HORIZONED BY RESURRECTION

Declared to be the Son of God with power, according to the spirit of holiness, by the resurrection from the dead (Romans 1:4).

THESE WORDS CONSTITUTE the second part of a double statement concerning one Person. That Person is indicated by a reference preceding the statement and by an explanation following it. The reference you will discover in the beginning of verse three: "concerning His Son." The explanation is contained in the closing part of verse four: "even Jesus Christ our Lord." Between this reference and this explanation we find the twofold statement concerning the Person thus referred to.

> Born of the seed of David according to the flesh.
> Declared to be the Son of God with power,
>> according to the spirit of holiness,
>> by the resurrection from the dead.

If for purposes of illumination, I may take from each of two parts of the words necessary to discover the simple contrast, we have this result. Paul says concerning this Person whom he first designates "Son of God" and finally refers to as "Jesus Christ our Lord," two things. First, according to the flesh He was "born of the seed of David." Secondly, according to the spirit He was "declared to be the Son of God with power . . . by the resurrection from the dead."

The first part of the apostolic declaration is simple and needs neither argument nor explanation, "of the seed of David, according to the flesh." The second part of the declaration was sublime and it was impossible—if I may thus interpret the method of the apostle—for him to write the second part without some qualification. "Of the seed of David according to the flesh," is a perfectly simple and natural declaration; but when he turns to the other side, "according to the spirit," he has to qualify, "according to the spirit of holiness;" or even more accurately as I think, "according to a *holy spirit*." "According to the flesh" He was of the seed of David, and Paul knew that no argument of that fact was needed. But, "according to the spirit," the essential matter in that human life, there was a difference. The spirit of this Person was holy. All the values of this differentiation are discovered when we reach the eighth chapter of the epistle. Therein the apostle is careful to distinguish between flesh and spirit in every life. In flesh, and in spirit, are the two sides of every human life. They were both present in the life of Jesus. His flesh was "born of the seed of David." His spirit must be described. It stands alone. There never was such another. It was a holy spirit, the spirit of holiness. In flesh He was absolutely of our humanity. In spirit also, and yet different. Numbered with transgressors, separated from sinners. In flesh, of our humanity. In spirit essentially the same, but in character different—holy.

The evidence of His being of the seed of David was abundant and convincing. The evidences of His being the Son of God were abundant but not convincing. The evidence did not convince because those who observed were incapable of judging, for they were spiritually blind. The men who looked at Jesus in the days of His flesh were quite capable of judging material things, fleshly things; they could trace genealogies, and discover racial traits; "according to the flesh, born of the seed of David."

According to the spirit—they said He was a gluttonous man and a wine-bibber, the friend of publicans and sinners. They did not know Him. They could not be sure of Him. The evidences of divine Sonship were those of holiness. His thoughts, His words, His deeds, all of them were the vehicles through which the essential and awful purity of God sounded and shone upon the ways of men. "When we shall see Him there is no beauty that we should desire Him" (Isa. 53:2). Not that He was devoid of beauty, but that men were so blind they could not see it. The evidences of fleshly relationship were abundant and convincing. The evidences of divine relationship were abundant, but not convincing, because men had lost their spiritual vision and were incapable of judgment. If you object to that interpretation, how do you find it in the world today? Is the man of the world of today capable of judging of the beauty of holiness? Is not the sanctified life still the sport of the worldly man? If you dare to season your daily speech with the salt that tells that you have traffic with eternity, the worldly man sees nothing beautiful in it. He shrugs his shoulders. That is the new method of persecution, seeing that the rack has gone out of fashion. He smiles, and perhaps holds you in contempt. Some of you hold the saints in contempt because you are blind and cannot discover the beauty of holiness.

How shall this Man be proven the Son of God as well as Son of man, seeing that the holiness of His spirit does not appeal to men? "Declared to be the Son of God with power, according to the spirit of holiness, by the resurrection from the dead" (Rom. 1:4). It is that declaration of the text which we are now to consider. In order to do so, confining ourselves entirely to this half of the great statement concerning the Person, we must carefully understand what this thing is that the apostle wrote. May I change the phrasing, not that I can improve upon it, but that sometimes by a change of words we are introduced to the meaning which we miss by very familiarity with the older formula. So I read the text thus, "Who was distinguished," and that word must not be taken in the general sense in which we speak of a man as being distinguished. "Who was *marked out* as the Son of God with power through the means of the resurrection of dead ones?"

May I further change the text, this time not by translation in other words, but by paraphrase. "The resurrection of dead ones set Him with powerful effect upon the horizon as the Son of God."

I do not suggest that that is the translation, so those of you who are reading from the Greek New Testament need not be anxious. I do not intend it as interpretation. Those of you who are familiar with the passage in the Greek will discover that I have dared to take a Greek word and Anglicize it. What is this word "declared," "distinguished," "marked out?" It is the word from which we have derived our word "horizon." What is the horizon? The boundary. What is a boundary? The end? By no means. It is the beginning. If only I could transport you to the sea, you would understand my text. Standing on the land's last limit there stretches the sea with its movement and its rhythm, its music and its laughter. What beyond? The horizon, the boundary. Is that the end? That is the beginning. Everything between me and the horizon I can comprehend. The mystery begins where the horizon bounds my vision. It is limitation. The limitation is only limitation of my vision, not of the essential fact. According to flesh, everyone can read the story, "born of the seed of David." According to the spirit, "*horizoned* as the Son of God by the resurrection of dead ones."

Resurrection demonstrated the essential truth concerning Him. Apart from the resurrection, He is "born of the seed of David;" a great and gracious fact, and no one imagines I am undervaluing it. My heart exults with the apostle John who handled Him. I am glad that men of my kith and kin nineteen hundred years ago did actually lay hands upon the warm flesh of the Man of Nazareth. That, however, is not all. That is not the final fact. If you make that the final fact, your Christianity will be a diminishing quantity, losing all its essential virtue and all its power of victory; until presently you will put Him by the side of Confucius, Buddha, and the rest; a sorry spectacle over which angels might weep.

There is something else. He is the Son of God according to the spirit of holiness; and He is demonstrated as such, horizoned as such, flaming out as the sun upon the horizon, and rising to meridian glory, by way of the resurrection. That is the supreme value of the resurrection. The resurrection is the unanswerable demonstration of the profoundest fact concerning the Christ, that, namely, of His divine Sonship.

In order to gain appreciation of this, let me take you very quickly along three lines of consideration. First, the truth that Jesus was the Son of God, as apprehended before the Resurrection. Second, the truth that Jesus was the Son of God, as apprehended after the Resurrection. Third, the Resurrection as the means of demonstration.

Christ's Sonship as Understood Before the Resurrection

First, the truth as apprehended before the resurrection. That is to say, I suggest that we shall, for a few minutes only, put ourselves back among the disciples before that event happened which we celebrate today.

I take up my New Testament and go through the gospel stories and find three titles of Jesus constantly recurring, "Son of Man," "Son of God," and "The Son," without qualification. I have nothing to do with the title "Son of Man." That put Him into immediate relationship with humanity. I take the title "Son of God." Please forgive the statistical way of stating this, I only desire to leave an impression upon your mind. It occurs in Matthew nine times, in Mark four times, in Luke six times, in John eleven times. Of course some of those occasions overlap, it does not all matter for my present purpose. I find in Matthew that He is called the Son of God six times by men, three times by devils. Mark records two occasions when men so designated Him, and two occasions when devils called Him "the Son of God." Luke gives one occasion when a man called Him that, and four when devils so named Him, and one when an angel declared Him to be the Son of God. I come to John and I find six occasions when man referred to Him as the Son of God, and five when He so named Himself.

Take the other title "The Son," more splendid perhaps than the other because of its independence of qualification. Adjectives are often the means of weakening the glory of substantives. The proportion in which we can use substantives alone, apart from adjectives, is the proportion of dignity of statement and suggestion. Matthew has the description "The Son" four times, Mark once, Luke three times, John fifteen times. That phrase, according to the records, never fell from the lips of devil, or man, or angel. It is the peculiar phrase of Jesus.

With these figures in your mind, let me take another survey of these gospels. Christ did claim for Himself, by direct use of the title and by constant assumptions of commonplace speech, that He was the veritable Son of God. That fact was attested in a supernatural way on two occasions, when heaven's silence was broken and the divine voice was heard. "This is My beloved Son, in Whom I am well pleased" so at baptism; "This is my beloved Son, in Whom I am well pleased; hear ye Him;" so on the holy mount. The fact was witnessed by devils, as when one said to Him, "I know Thee who Thou art, the Holy One of God," and another "Thou art the Son of God," and yet another "What have I to do with Thee, Jesus, Thou Son of the Most High God? I adjure Thee by God, torment me not." That fact was once confessed by a man amid the rocky fastnesses of Caesarea Philippi, when answering the challenge of Christ Himself he said, "Thou art the Christ, the Son of the living God."

If you will go over these occasions, I can but suggest the line, you will find that every confession of Sonship was closely associated with the thought of holiness. "My Son, in Whom I am well pleased," that is the declaration of His holiness. "I and the Father are one." "I do nothing of Myself, but as the Father taught Me, I speak these things. . . . I do always the things that are pleasing to Him," all that is the claim of holiness. "Thou art the Holy One of God," "Thou art the Son of God;" so evil recognized His holiness. and surely you will agree that Peter meant that when He said "Thou art," not the prophet foretelling, but the Messiah fulfilling.

That is a rapid survey of those days prior to the Resurrection. What shall we say of it? The fact of His divine Sonship was breaking on the consciousness of men. It was only the flush of dawn upon the dark sky. Men did not know Him as the Son of God. Peter confessed Him as the Son of God, but immediately afterwards rebuked Him, and by his rebuke demonstrated the fact that he had no full conception of the thing he had said. There he lived amongst men, holy, undefiled, spotless, pure, the Son of God; and they were puzzled, they wondered, but they did not fully comprehend.

Christ's Sonship as Understood
After the Resurrection

Turn over the New Testament to the remaining part of it. How far was the truth of the divine Sonship apprehended after the Resurrection? To an audience such as I am addressing this morning, the inquiry carries its own answer. We know full well that all the thought of the other writings of the New Testament is saturated with the conception of the divine Sonship of Jesus. It was the central conviction concerning Him. It was the constant reason of loyalty to Him. It was the persistent burden of testimony concerning Him. I will not weary you with saying things about that conviction. Let me rather end this section of our study with two quotations: "Who is the image of the invisible God, the firstborn of all creation; for in Him were all things created, in the heavens and upon the earth, things visible and things invisible, whether thrones, or dominions, or principalities, or powers; all things have been created through Him, and unto Him; and He is before all things, and in Him all things consist" (Col. 1:15-17).

That is the vision of Jesus Christ which flamed upon the consciousness of believing men after the resurrection.

Or, take another quotation which you may consider anonymous or which you may attribute to the same pen, I care not: "God, having of old time spoken unto the fathers in the prophets by divers portions and in divers manners, hath at the end of these days spoken unto us in His Son, Whom He appointed heir of all things, through Whom also He made the worlds; Who being the brightness of His glory, and the very image of His substance, and upholding all things by the word of His power, when He had made purification of sins, sat down on the right hand of the Majesty on high" (Heb. 1:1-3).

I go back to these men before the Resurrection and see that gleams were upon the sky. To repeat my own figure of speech, the flush of the dawn was upon the sky, but it was twilight. They were not sure.

On the other side of the Resurrection, the sun is in the heavens shining in full glory. Christ is horizoned as the Son of God with power by the resurrection of dead ones, not by His own resurrection only, but by the resurrection of dead ones.

Let us go back again to the period before His cross. I have three stories of His raising the dead. First, the widow's son. What effect did that miracle produce? The people glorified God; they said, God has visited His people. They had not come to final doctrinal understanding of the Person of the Man who had wrought the work, but when He raised the dead they said, God has visited us.

The resurrection of the son of the widow of Nain was evidence to them of the divine presence, the divine visitation, and therefore of holiness. When He raised the widow's son, a great man was in prison, "among them that are born of women there hath not arisen a greater than John the Baptist." He had changed all the inspiration of a great public ministry which made kings tremble—for Herod heard him gladly at one time—for the dungeon and loneliness and questioning. I cannot help feeling that he had come to wonder whether, after all that, Jesus of Nazareth whom he had named, was the actual One; but when he heard this, that one was raised from the dead, he sent his disciples to ask, "Art Thou He that should come, or look we for another?" It was this supreme miracle of resurrection which renewed questioning, wonder, hope, in his mind. Then presently He raised the daughter of Jairus in that inimitable word spoken, thrilling with the power of Deity: "Little darling, arise." The parents were amazed. That is all, but that is much. Amazed, they had touched the consciousness of power beyond the reach of humanity. Once again, Lazarus is dead, and they bring Him the news. What is His own account of the fact that He did not hurry, that He permitted Lazarus to die? This is it. "That the Son of God might be glorified thereby." "Declared to be the Son of God, with power . . . by the resurrection of dead ones." That is the supreme revelation. That is the supreme miracle.

But what next? The Cross. What did that mean? All the fitful gleams of light which had been shining through Judaea, Peraea and Galilee, all the flush of dawning upon the eastern sky which the eager watchers had seen, went out, and never a ray of light remained. The sun was eclipsed in blood. According to the flesh, oh yes, we knew Him well, "Born of the seed of David," the genealogy is complete. We hoped, when He raised the daughter of Jairus, and the widow's son, and Lazarus, that He was more, but He is dead. You know the rest. We celebrate it this morning. He arose from among the dead. Many infallible proofs for forty days. He is horizoned. Horizoned as the Son of God.

> Lo, our sun's eclipse is o'er.
> Hallelujah!
> Lo, He sets in blood no more!
> Hallelujah!

The Resurrection as a Demonstration of Christ's Sonship

The Resurrection was the vindication of every claim He made; the demonstration of His Sonship; the revelation of His holiness.

According to flesh, "born of the seed of David." We can be accurate. According to the spirit of holiness, Who is He? There is only one way in which it can be proven, and that is by the resurrection of the dead ones. The son of the widow of Nain, the daughter of Jairus, and Lazarus. Yes, but He died. But He is alive forevermore. Take that away from me, my masters, and I renounce your bastard Christianity. I have no hope if that be not so. "If Christ hath not been raised, then is our preaching vain, your faith also is vain . . . ye are yet in your sins" (1 Cor. 15:14, 17). Blessed be God, why such supposition? He arose, and is alive!

The final demonstration is not yet. I am not coming to the supreme value of the plural in my text. "Horizoned as the Son of God, marked out as the Son of God, with power . . . by the resurrection of dead ones." The final demonstration will never be until the Advent, when not only the first fruits, but all the company are with Him, "the resurrection of dead ones."

> Ten thousand times ten thousand,
> In sparkling raiment bright,

The armies of the ransomed saints
Throng up the steeps of light;
'Tis finished—all is finished
Their fight with death and sin!
Fling open wide the golden gates,
And let the victors in.

What rush of Hallelujahs
Fills all the earth and sky!
What ringing of a thousand harps
Bespeaks the triumphs nigh!
Oh, day, for which creation
And all its tribes were made!
Oh, Joy, for all its former woes
A thousandfold repaid!

The final demonstration will be in the resurrection of the saints. So that the resurrection of the saints is not the last thing, it is the beginning. Do not limit God and humanity by the end of this age, or by the millennium. Everything so far has been preparatory. Stretching away beyond me, I dream dreams of unborn ages and new creations, and marvelous processions out of the being of God, but through them all, the risen Christ and the risen saints will be the central revelations of holiness and of life.

That is the glory of the final resurrection. As so often, we leave the subject, not that it is exhausted. Suffer me this final word. The fact of His divine Sonship demonstrated by the resurrection is the rock of our assurance. Said a man imperfectly knowing what he said, "Thou art the Christ, the Son of the living God." Answered Christ, "Upon this rock I will build My church." The rock foundation of the Christian church is this fact of His divine Sonship, and so essential Deity lies beneath the church, an impregnable rock. Thank God if we are built thereupon by sharing the very nature of this risen One.

Let us go away this morning rejoicing in the resurrection because it is the message of a great confidence. He is King, Priest, Warrior, and Builder, and all the great relationships are linked to His resurrection because He is demonstrated thereby as the Son of God.

His Kingship is an absolute monarchy. I have no anxiety about His reign. I believe in an absolute monarchy when we can find the right King. We have found Him.

As to His prophetic mission, it is one of absolute authority. What He said is true. It cannot be gainsaid. All the words gathered from His tender lips, and printed here and preserved for us, are words which abide. "Heaven and earth shall pass away, but My word shall not pass away." I have no intellectual quarrel with anything He says.

As to His priesthood, the resurrection demonstrates its absolute sufficiency. Do you really believe that? Then why do you grieve God by this perpetual grieving over sin, and the declaration that you cannot believe He can forgive you?

> Grace there is my every debt to pay,
> Blood to wash my every sin away.

I know it because the Priest rose and entered in.

As to His triumph, He hath broken in pieces the gates of brass. He hath cut the bars of iron asunder. He hath triumphed gloriously, and He will win His battle and build His city. Then so help me God, as He will permit me, I fain would share the travail that makes His kingdom come, entering the fellowship of His sufferings, for all the while the light of His resurrection is upon the pathway, and I know that at the last the things which He has made me suffer will be the things of the unending triumph.

I greet you this morning in the name of the Father, and of the Son, and of the Holy Spirit! Seek not the living among the dead. He is risen, and because He is risen, we shall rise, and His victory and ours will be won.

The Road to Emmaus

George H. Morrison (1866-1928) assisted the great
Alexander Whyte in Edinburgh, Scotland, pastored two
churches, and then became a pastor in 1902 of the
distinguished Wellington Church on University Avenue
in Glasgow, Scotland. His preaching drew great crowds;
in fact, people had to line up an hour before the services
to be sure to get seats in the large auditorium. Morrison
is a master of imagination in preaching, yet his messages
are solidly biblical.

From his many published volumes of sermons, I have
chosen this message from *The Weaving of Glory*,
published by Hodder and Stoughton, London.

George H. Morrison

9

THE ROAD TO EMMAUS

Two of them went that same day to a village called Emmaus (Luke 24:13-35).

OF ALL THE appearances of the risen Christ, none has a stronger hold upon Christendom than this one. It has brought light to many darkened hearts, and comfort to innumerable souls. Christ revealed Himself to Mary in the garden, and that will always be precious to the church. He revealed Himself to the eleven, and to Thomas, and to Peter and John beside the sea of Galilee. But this meeting on the Emmaus road, with its revelation of the living Savior, is engraven on universal heart.

Who these two were we cannot tell. We know nothing about them except the name of one of them. And we are not at liberty to associate that name *Cleophas* with the *Klopas* who is mentioned in the gospels. That they were not of the eleven disciples is certain, for it was to the eleven that they hurried with their news. They were clearly on intimate terms with the apostles, for they knew where they lodged when they went straight to them. But beyond that we know nothing of the men, neither their story in the days before the cross, nor yet their service in the coming years when the Holy Spirit was given at Pentecost. They were in no sense distinguished persons. They were not outstanding in their zeal or love. They occupied no place of proud pre-eminence among those who had been followers of the Lord. And I take it as characteristic of the Lord that in the glory of His resurrection-life He gave Himself with such fullness of disclosure to those unknown and undistinguished men. It reminds one vividly of that earlier hour when He had talked with the woman of Samaria. She too was nameless, and utterly obscure, yet with *her* had He lingered in the richest converse. And now the cross has come, and He has died and risen, yet being risen He is still unchanged, for He still reveals Himself to lowly hearts. Here is the Savior for the common man. Here is the Lord who does not spurn the humble. Here is the Master of all those obscure lives that are yet precious in the sight of heaven. Had these two travelers been John and Peter, we might have hesitated to take home their rich experience, but being what they were, they are our brothers.

The Spiritual Condition of the Two

First, then, let us try to understand the state of mind of these two travelers. And in the first place this is notable, that *these two travelers had lost their hopes*. There was a time, not so long ago, when their hopes had been burning brightly like a star. They trusted this was He who should redeem Israel—that was the glowing conviction of their hearts. And as they followed Jesus in His public ministry, and saw His miracles, and heard His words, brighter and ever brighter grew the hope that this was the Christ, the Son of the living God. Even the cross itself had not dispelled their hopes, for they remembered that He had talked of that. They remembered that He had said, "Destroy this temple, and in three days I will raise it up again" (John 2:19). But now the third day's sun was near to setting, and darkness was soon to fall upon the world, and a great darkness, heavier than sunset, was beginning to cast its shadow on their hearts. It was true that some women had come hurrying in, bearing the tidings that the tomb was empty. But it was one thing to be told the tomb was empty, and quite another to believe that Christ was risen. And even the women had confessed, when questioned, that they had not seen the Lord Himself, but only an empty grave, and the stone rolled away, and certain mysterious shapes they took for angels. Clearly, then, their Master had not risen. He was still sleeping somewhere beneath that Syrian sky. They would never see Him again, nor hear His words, nor follow Him through any village street. And so that evening, journeying to Emmaus, they were men convinced that they had lost their Lord, and having lost Him they had lost their hopes. Are there any here who are like these men?—any who have lost their hope in Christ? Any to whom Christ was very real once, and who now have a name to live and yet are dead? My brother and sister, if that be your condition— if once you had a hope that now is dimmed—you are like these two journeying to Emmaus.

Then, in the next place this is notable, that these *two travelers had lost their gladness.* "What are you speaking of," said Jesus to them, "as ye walk together *and are sad?*" (Luke 24:17). Sometimes, as we pass along the streets, we meet a face of unutterable sadness. Sorrow is stamped on every lineament of it, all the more tragic because a smile is there. And when we see it, amid the crowd of faces that bear no trace of any great experience, it haunts us so that it is long ere we forget it. Now that is what our Lord seems to have noticed, graven deep upon the faces of these travelers. "What are ye talking about," He said to them, "as ye joy walk together and are sad?" The utter absence of joy upon their face—the look of melancholy and of sorrow—touched at once His tender loving heart. And can you wonder that their looks were sad, when all that brightened life for them was gone? A hopeless heart may be a very brave heart, but I never heard that it was a merry heart. So these two disciples, having lost their hopes, had lost their gladness which is the child of hope, and as they walked together they were sad.

So long as Jesus Christ had been alive, there had been a great gladness in their hearts. Only to see Him had been like music to them, as it always is with any one we love. That they had had their troubles just like other people, is only to say that they were human. Perhaps they were farmers struggling with short harvests, or fishermen who had often toiled and had caught nothing. But this was certain, that in Jesus' company their deepest experience was a great gladness, a joy that they never could quite fathom, and yet which they knew to be intensely real. Always in His society there was delight. There was a feeling of peace and of security. When He was with them all their care and worry took to itself wings and fled away. But now their Lord has passed beyond their ken, and it was like the passing of the sunshine for them, and as they walked together they were sad.

Now sadness is of many kinds. There is the sadness which the exile feels when he is far away from home and kindred, and when in the thronging of the crowd around him he catches no glimpse of a familiar face. There is the sadness which the aged feel, when they remember happy days now gone forever; and there is the sadness of the open grave. All these are elements of our mortality, but there is a spiritual sadness different from these, and the cause of it is an absent Lord. When in prayer the heavens seem as brass, when the Bible loses its fragrance and its dew, when spiritual books begin to pall on us, when the services of the House of God become a weariness, then is the heart of the true disciple sad. Then does one feel as if Jesus had not risen, and as if all one's hopes in Him had been a mockery. Then do men cry the exceeding bitter cry, "They have taken away my Lord, and I know not where they have laid Him." And should there be any of God's children here this evening who are suffering from such spiritual desertion, I beg of them to remember that their frame of heart is like that of the two journeying to Emmaus.

But there is one thing more that is notable, and it is this, that these *two had lost none of their desire*. They had lost their hope and they had lost their gladness, but they had lost none of their desire. That afternoon, walking to Emmaus, their talk was all of the Lord Jesus Christ. And from a hint in the original, we learn that their talk was animated, intense, and eager. They were talking loudly, as Orientals do, and the words were being flung one to the other, for out of the fullness of the heart the mouth was speaking. Some one has said, and there is truth in it, that our friends are never really ours till we have lost them. Only then, undimmed and unobscured, does the vision of them arise within our hearts. And as it is with those whom we have loved, and who have left us and passed into the shadow, so was it with these disciples and their Lord. They never understood how much they needed Him until the day when they thought that He was gone. They never understood how much they loved Him, till the shadow of parting had fallen on their love. But now they knew it, and so, that dreary day, their talk as they journeyed was all of Jesus Christ, and the deepest desire of their hearts was this: O that I knew where I might find Him! Are there any here this evening who in the secret of their souls are saying that? Careless and prayerless, backsliding and worldly, are you coming to feel you cannot live without Him? If so—if as the hart for the water-brooks, unsatisfied, you thirst for the living God—remember you have a kinship with these two.

Such then was the spiritual condition of these men, and now we want to know how Jesus dealt with them. We want to follow the successive stages by which He gave them back their joy and peace.

How Christ Dealt With Them

In the first place, then, and passing by minor matters, *He showed them the supreme necessity of His death.* "Ought not Christ," He said, "to have suffered these things, that so He might enter into glory?" (Luke 24:26). We may take it for certain that these two disciples had never really grasped the need that Christ should die. They had shared in the common hope that He would reign, and it was a throne they were dreaming of and not a cross. If any dark surmisings had arisen in them, stirred by the mysterious words of Jesus, they had crushed them as something too terrible to contemplate. That He whom they loved should die a felon's death was something too awful to believe. And when it happened—there, before their eyes—it seemed a hideous and irreparable calamity. It was as if there had been some mistake in heaven; as if the will of the Eternal had been baffled; as if powers were abroad defying the Messiah, and hurrying His triumph into tragedy. And then Christ met them, and spoke about His death, and they learned that the crucifixion was no accident. It was no longer the greatest of calamities; it became the greatest of necessities. Ought not Christ to have suffered these things?—and they saw its moral and spiritual grandeur, and it dawned upon them that the cross they loathed was something more wonderful than any crown. It was *then* that their hearts began to burn within them, and the light to break upon their darkened souls. And everything looked different to them now when they saw the meaning of the death of Jesus. And I venture to say that it is always so with hearts that are hungering for the living God—the primary step towards fellowship and peace is to come face to face with the death of Jesus Christ. That I am a sinner and cannot save myself—that God has provided an all-sufficient Savior—that He has died for me, and that I die in Him, and through His death reach up to heaven again,—all this, so simple that a child can grasp it, and yet so deep that angels cannot fathom it, is the basis of our peace with God. Think not to comprehend all that it means. The deepest we can never comprehend. Call it a substitution if you will—call it an atonement, call it anything. The vital thing is not what you may call it; the vital thing is to grasp it and to feel it, and feeling it to find that in the blood of Christ there is peace of conscience and fellowship with God.

Then the next step our Savior took was to lead *them back to the Word of God again*. "Beginning at Moses and at all the prophets, He expounded unto them the things concerning Himself" (Luke 24:27). We know from the gospels how Christ had loved the Scripture in the days of His ministry before the cross. We know how He used it when He was tempted, and how He preached from it in the synagogue of Nazareth. And it is a sign to us that He is still the same, though He has passed into the resurrection glory, that He still goes back to the old familiar Scripture which He had learned beside His mother's knee. It is a singular thing that, after He was risen, Christ never once appeared to His mother. The name of Mary is never mentioned once in the forty days of our Savior's resurrection. But I sometimes think that when she heard these two rehearsing all that He had taught them from the Scriptures, she would have her own sweet secret memories of the old home, and would be quietly certain she was not forgotten. Had these two travelers, then, been neglecting their Bibles? I do not think that that is the least likely. Probably they knew Moses and the prophets far better than any of us in church tonight. But I want you to think what Scripture must have meant to them in all manner of unexpected depth and fullness, when the interpreter of it was the Lord Jesus Christ.

You and I may have listened to some saintly preacher drawing out the inner meaning of God's Word. And as we did so, our hearts burned within us, and we saw what we had never seen before. And if that be so with an erring, sinful minister, I want you to try to think what it must have been when the risen Son of God handled the Scripture, and showed these two the meaning of it all. Once again they heard of the Paschal Lamb, and of the Brazen Serpent in the wilderness, and of the smitten shepherd in Zechariah, and of the suffering servant in Isaiah. But hearing it all interpreted by Christ, the Bible became a living book to them, and in the hour when it became a living book, they found that Christ Himself was by their side. Once more do I venture to suggest that it is always so in the experience of the soul.

One of the surest signs that Christ is nigh is when He makes the Bible live again. It is a living Christ who makes a living Scripture, and when He is going to reveal Himself to us, passages that we have known since we were children begin once to live and burn for us. If Christ be absent, then all the lore of ages will never make the Word a living book. If Christ be dead for us, in heart and conscience, then is the Bible always a dead book. But when old texts take a strange grip of us, when they haunt us through the market and the street, when we cannot silence some gracious invitation, when we cannot shake off some oracle of warning, when promises come like music to our ear in days of despondency or hours of peril, when some great text that we have long ignored reaches out its loving hands to us,—I say that when *that* happens to a man, the risen Savior is not far away. That was what the two disciples found. The Bible became a living book to them. And their hearts burned within them as they heard again the echo of the old familiar passages. And it all meant that He whom they thought vanished was not vanished but at their very side, though their eyes were holden, and they did not know Him.

And then *He revealed Himself in the breaking of the bread*, and it seems like an anti-climax, does it not? After all this marshaled preparation, shall we not look for something far more glorious? We shall have some vision that will strike the senses? We shall have some flash of glory on the eye? "And He revealed Himself in the breaking of the bread." It was in no sense a sacramental meal, as we use that word sacrament in our theology. It was a frugal supper in a village home of two tired travelers, and another. Yet it was then—in the breaking of the bread, and not in any vision of resurrection splendor—that they knew that companion was the Lord. How that discovery flashed upon their hearts, the Bible, so wonderful in its silences, does not tell. It may have been the quiet air of majesty with which He took at once the place of host, when they had invited Him in to be their guest. It may have been the familiar word of blessing that awakened sweet memories of Galilean days. Or it may have been that as He put forth His hand after the blessing to take the bread and break it, they saw that it was a hand which had been pierced. However it was, whether by word or hand, they felt irresistibly that this was He. Some little action, some dear familiar trait, told them in a flash this was the Christ. Not in some vision of resurrection-glory, but in some characteristic movement of the fingers, maybe, they recognized that they found their Lord.

In daily life we are always meeting that—the revelation of the insignificant. A certain trick of speech—a tone, a look—and some one whom we have lost is at our side again. And so when a man has spiritually lost his Savior, and is being restored to the joy of his first love, it is often so that the Lord reveals Himself. Our commonest mercies come to gleam on us as the most wonderful of all created things. Our sicknesses, our trials, our disappointments are all transfigured with a Father's love. Until at last though we have seen no vision, and have only had common

meals and common mercies, we too are thrilled and say,
"It is the Lord." When that deep certainty once fills a man
it seems as if nothing else could ever matter. When that
deep certainty once fills a man, in a real sense for him to
live is Christ. When that deep certainty once fills a man
he will hurry like these two disciples to Jerusalem, and
tell out, though he may not say a word, that he has seen
the Lord.

The Resurrection of Our Lord Jesus

Charles Haddon Spurgeon (1834-1892) is undoubtedly the most famous minister of modern times. Converted in 1850, he united with the Baptists and soon began to preach in various places. He became pastor of the Baptist church in Waterbeach in 1851, and three years later he was called to the decaying Park Street Church, London. Within a short time, the work began to prosper, a new church was built and dedicated in 1861, and Spurgeon became London's most popular preacher. In 1855, he began to publish his sermons weekly; and today they make up the fifty-seven volumes of *The Metropolitan Tabernacle Pulpit*. He founded a pastor's college and several orphanages.

This sermon is taken from *The Metropolitan Tabernacle Pulpit*, volume 28. He preached it on Sunday morning, April 9, 1882.

Charles Haddon Spurgeon

10

THE RESURRECTION OF OUR LORD JESUS

Remember that Jesus Christ of the seed of David was raised from the dead according to my gospel (2 Timothy 2:8).

FROM LONG SICKNESS my mind is scarcely equal to the work before me. Certainly, if I had ever sought after brilliance of thought or language, I should have failed today, for I am almost at the lowest stage of incapacity. I have only been comforted in the thought of preaching to you this morning by the reflection that it is the doctrine itself which God blesses, and not the way in which it may be spoken; for if God had made the power to depend upon the speaker and his style, he would have chosen that the Resurrection, grandest of all truths, should have been proclaimed by angels rather than by men. Yet he set aside the seraph for the humbler creature. After angels had spoken a word or two to the women their testimony ceased. The most prominent testimony to the resurrection of the Lord was at the first that of holy women, and afterwards that of each one of the guileless men and women who made up the five hundred or more whose privilege it was to have actually seen the risen Savior, and who therefore could bear witness to what they had seen, though they may have been quite unable to describe with eloquence what they had beheld. Upon our Lord's rising I having nothing to say, and God's ministers have nothing to say, beyond bearing witness to the fact that Jesus Christ of the seed of David was raised from the dead. Put it in poetry, tell it out in sublime Miltonic verse, it will come to no more; tell it out in monosyllables, and write it so that little children may read it in their first spelling-books, and it will come to nothing less. "The Lord is risen indeed" is the sum and substance of our witness when we speak of our risen Redeemer. If we do but know the truth of this resurrection, and feel the power of it, our mode of utterance is of secondary consequence; for the Holy Spirit will bear witness to the truth, and cause it to produce fruit in the minds of our hearers.

Our present text is found in Paul's second letter to Timothy. The venerable minister is anxious about the young man who has preached with remarkable success, and whom he regards in some respects as his successor. The old man is about to put off his tabernacle, and he is concerned that his son in the gospel, should preach the same truth as his father has preached, and should by no means adulterate the gospel. A tendency showed itself in Timothy's day, and the same tendency exists at this very hour, to try to get away from the simple matters of fact upon which our religion is built, to something more philosophical and hard to be understood. The word which the common people heard gladly is not fine enough for cultured sages, so they must needs surround it with a mist of human thought and speculation. Three or four plain facts constitute the gospel, even as Paul puts it in the fifteenth chapter of his first epistle to the Corinthians: "For I delivered unto you first of all that which I also received, how that Christ died for our sins according to the Scriptures; and that he was buried, and that he rose again the third day according to the Scriptures."

Upon the incarnation, life, death and resurrection of Jesus our salvation hinges. He who believes these truths aright hath believed the gospel, and believing the gospel he shall without doubt find eternal salvation therein. But men want novelties; they cannot endure that the trumpet should give forth the same certain sound, they crave some fresh fantasia every day. "The *gospel with variations*" is the music for them. Intellect is progressive, they say; they must, therefore, march ahead of their forefathers. Incarnate Deity, a holy life, an atoning death, and a literal resurrection,—having heard these things now for nearly nineteen centuries they are just a little stale, and the cultivated mind hungers for a change from the old-fashioned manna. Even in Paul's day this tendency was manifest, and so they sought to regard facts as mysteries or parables, and they labored to find a spiritual meaning in them till they went so far as to deny them as actual facts. Seeking a recondite meaning, they overlooked the fact itself, losing the substance in a foolish preference for the shadow. While God set before them glorious events which fill heaven with amazement they showed their foolish wisdom by accepting the plain historical facts as myths to be interpreted or riddles to be solved. He who believed as a little child was pushed aside as a fool that the disputer and the scribe might come in to mystify simplicity, and hid the light of truth. Hence there had arisen a certain Hymenaeus and Philetus, "who concerning the truth have erred, saying that the resurrection is past already; and overthrow the faith of some" (2 Tim. 2:18). They spirited away the resurrection; they made it to mean something very deep and mystical, and in the process they took away the actual resurrection altogether.

Among men there is still a craving after new meanings, refinements upon old doctrines, and spiritualizations of literal facts. They tear out the bowels of the truth, and give us the carcass stuffed with hypotheses, speculations, and larger hopes. The golden shields of Solomon are taken away, and shields of brass are hung up in their stead: will they not answer every purpose, and is not the metal more in favor with the age? It may be so, but we never admired Rehoboam, and we are old-fashioned enough to prefer the original shields of gold. The apostle Paul was very anxious that Timothy at least should stand firm to the old witness, and should understand in their plain meaning his testimonies to the fact that Jesus Christ of the seed of David rose again from the dead.

Within the compass of this verse several facts are recorded: and, first, there is here the great truth that *Jesus, the Son of the Highest, was anointed of God*; the apostle calls him "Jesus *Christ*" that is, the anointed one, the Messiah, the sent of God. He calls him also *"Jesus,"* which signifies a Savior, and it is a grand truth that he who was born of Mary, he who was laid in the manger at

Bethlehem, he who loved and lived and died for us, is the ordained and anointed Savior of men. We have not a moment's doubt about the mission, office, and design of our Lord Jesus; in fact, we hang our soul's salvation upon his being anointed of the Lord to be the Savior of men.

This *Jesus Christ was really and truly man*; for Paul says he was *"of the seed of David."* True He was divine, and His birth was not after the ordinary manner of men, but still He was in all respects partaker of our human nature, and came of the stock of David. This also we do believe. We are not among those who spiritualize the incarnation, and suppose that God was here as a phantom, or that the whole story is but an instructive legend. Nay, in very flesh and blood did the Son of God abide among men: bone of our bone and flesh of our flesh was He in the days of His sojourn here below. We know and believe that Jesus Christ has come in the flesh. We love the incarnate God, and in Him we fix our trust.

It is implied, too, in the text that *Jesus died*; for He could not be raised from the dead if He had not first gone down among the dead, and been one of them. Yes, Jesus died: the crucifixion was no delusion, the piercing of His side with a spear was most clear and evident proof that He was dead: His heart was pierced, and the blood and water flowed therefrom. As a dead man He was taken down from the cross and carried by gentle hands, and laid in Joseph's virgin tomb. I think I see that pale corpse, white as a lily. Mark how it is distained with the blood of His five wounds, which make Him red as the rose. See how the holy women tenderly wrap Him in fine linen with sweet spices, and leave Him to spend His sabbath all alone in the rock-hewn sepulcher. No man in this world was ever more surely dead than He. "He made His grave with the wicked and with the rich in His death" (Isa. 53:9). As dead they laid him in the place of the dead, with napkin and grave-clothes, and habiliments fit for a grave: then they rolled the great stone at the grave's mouth and left Him, knowing that He was dead.

Then comes the grand truth, that as soon as ever the third sun commenced His shining circuit *Jesus rose again*.

His body had not decayed, for it was not possible for that holy thing to see corruption; but still it had been dead; and by the power of God—by His own power, by the Father's power, by the power of the Spirit—for it is attributed to each of these in turn, before the sun had risen His dead body was quickened. The silent heart began again to beat, and through the stagnant canals of the veins the life-flood began to circulate. The soul of the Redeemer again took possession of the body, and it lived once more. There He was within the sepulcher, as truly living as to all parts of Him as He had ever been. He literally and truly, in a material body, came forth from the tomb to live among men till the hour of His ascension into heaven. This is the truth which is still to be taught, refine it who may, spiritualize it who dare. This is the historical fact which the apostles witnessed; this is the truth for which the confessors bled and died. This is the doctrine which is the key-stone of the arch of Christianity, and they that hold it not have cast aside the essential truth of God. How can they hope for salvation for their souls if they do not believe that "the Lord is risen indeed"?

This morning I wish to do three things. First, let us *consider the bearings of the resurrection of Christ upon the great truths*; secondly, let us consider *the bearings of this fact upon the gospel*, for it has such bearings, according to the text—Jesus Christ of the seed of David was raised from the dead according to my gospel;" thirdly, let us *consider its bearings on ourselves*, which are all indicated in the word, "Remember."

Bearings of the Resurrection Upon Other Great Truths

First, then, beloved, as God shall help us, let us consider the bearings of the fact that Jesus rose from the dead.

It is clear at the outset that *the resurrection of our Lord was a tangible proof that there is another life.* Have you not quoted a great many times certain lines about "that undiscovered country from whose borne no traveler returns"? It is not so. There was once a traveler who said that "I go to prepare a place for you, and if I go away I will come again and receive you unto myself; that where I am there ye may be also." He said, "A little time and ye shall see me, and again a little time and ye shall not see me, and because I go the Father" (John 14:3, 19). Do you not remember these words of His? Our divine Lord went to the undiscovered country, and He returned. He said that at the third day He would be back again, and He was true to His word. There is no doubt that there is another state for human life, for Jesus has been in it, and has come back from it. We have no doubt as to a future existence, for Jesus existed after death. We have no doubt as to a paradise of future bliss, for Jesus went to it and returned. Though He has left us again, yet that coming back to tarry with us forty days has given us a sure pledge that He will return a second time when the hour is due, and then will be with us for a thousand years, and reign on earth amongst His ancients gloriously. His return from among the dead is a pledge to us of existence after death, and we rejoice in it.

His resurrection is also a pledge that the body will surely live again and rise to a superior condition; for the body of our blessed Master was no phantom after death any more than before. "Handle me, and see."

Oh wondrous proof! He said, "Handle me, and see;" and then to Thomas, "Reach hither thy finger, and behold my hands; and reach hither thy hand, and thrust it into my side" (John 20:27). What deception is possible here? The risen Jesus was no mere spirit. He promptly cried, "A spirit hath not flesh and bones, as ye see me have." "Bring me," said He, "something to eat;" and as if to show how real His body was, though He did not need to eat, yet He did eat, and a piece of a broiled fish and of an honeycomb were proofs of the reality of the act. Now, the body of our Lord in its risen state did not exhibit the whole of His glorification; for otherwise we should have seen John falling at His feet as dead, and we should have seen all His disciples overcome with the glory of the vision; but, still, in a great measure, we may call the forty days' sojourn— "The life of Jesus in His glory upon earth." He was no longer despised and rejected of men; but a glory surrounded

Him. It is evident that the raised body passed from place to place in a single moment, that it appeared and vanished at will, and was superior to the laws of matter. The risen body was incapable of pain, of hunger, thirst, and weariness during the time in which it remained here below,—fit representative of the bulk of which it was the first-fruits. Of our body also it shall be said ere long, "It was sown in weakness, it is raised in power: it was sown in dishonor, it is raised in glory" (1 Cor. 15:43, 44). Let us, then, as we think of the risen Christ, rest quite sure of a future life, and quite sure that our body will exist in it in a glorified condition.

I do not know whether you are ever troubled with doubts in connection with the world to come as to whether it can be true that we shall live eternally. Here is the respect which makes death so terrible to doubters; for while they have realized the grave, they have not realized the life beyond it. Now, the best help to that realization is a firm grip of the fact that Jesus died and Jesus rose again. This fact is proved better than any other event in history; the witness to it is far stronger than to anything else that is written either in profane or sacred records. The rising of our Lord Jesus Christ being certain, you may rest assured of the existence of another world. That is the first bearing of this great truth.

Secondly, Christ's *rising from the dead was the seal to all His claims.* It was true, then, that He was sent of God, for God raised Him from the dead in confirmation of His mission. He had said himself, "Destroy this body, and in three days I will raise it up." Lo, there He is: the temple of His body is rebuilt! He had even given this as a sign, that as Jonah was three days and three nights in the whale's belly, so should the Son of man be three days and three nights in the heart of the earth, and should then come forth to life again. Behold His own appointed sign fulfilled! Before men's eye the seal is manifest! Suppose Christ had never risen. You and I might have believed in the truth of a certain mission which God had given Him; but we could never have believed in the truth of such a commission as He claimed to have received—a commission to be our Redeemer from death and hell. How could He be our ransom from the grave if He had himself remained under the dominion of death?

Dear friends, the rising of Christ from the dead proved that this man was innocent of every sin. He could not be holden by the bands of death, for there was no sin to make those bands fast. Corruption could not touch His pure body, for no original sin had defiled the Holy One. Death could not keep Him a continual prisoner, because He had not actually come under sin; and though He took sin of ours, and bore it by imputation, and therefore died, yet He had no fault of His own, and must, therefore, be set free when His imputed load had been removed.

Moreover, Christ's rising from the dead proved His claim to Deity. We are told in another place that He was proved to be the Son of God with power by the resurrection from the dead. He raised himself by His own power, and though the Father and the Holy Spirit were cooperative with Him, and hence His resurrection is ascribed to them, yet it was because the Father had given Him to have life in himself, that therefore He arose from the dead. Oh, risen Savior, thy rising is the seal of thy work! We can have no doubt about thee now that thou hast left the tomb. Prophet of Nazareth, thou art indeed the Christ of God, for God has loosed the bands of death for thee! Son of David, thou art indeed the elect and precious One, for thou ever livest! Thy resurrection life has set the sign-manual of heaven to all that thou hast said and done, and for this we bless and magnify thy name.

A third bearing of His resurrection is this, and it is a very grand one,—*The resurrection of our Lord, according to the Scripture, was the acceptance of His sacrifice.* By the Lord Jesus Christ rising from the dead evidence was given that He had fully endured the penalty which was due to human guilt. "The soul that sinneth it shall die" (Ezek. 18:20)—that is the determination of the God of heaven. Jesus stands in the sinner's stead and dies: and when he has done *that* nothing more can be demanded of him, for he that is dead is free from the law. You take a man who has been guilty of a capital offense: he is condemned to be hanged, he is hanged by the neck till he is dead—what more has the law to do with him? It has done with him, for it has executed its sentence upon him; if he can be brought back to life again he is clear from the law; no writ that runs in Her Majesty's dominions can touch him—he has suffered the penalty. So when our Lord Jesus rose from the dead, after having died, He had fully paid the penalty that was due to justice for the sin of His people, and his new life was a life clear of penalty, free from liability. You and I are clear from the claims of the law because Jesus stood in our stead, and God will not exact payment both from us and from our Substitute: it were contrary to justice to sue both the Surety and those for whom He stood. And now, joy upon joy! the burden of liability which once did lie upon the Substitute is removed from Him also; seeing He has by the suffering of death vindicated justice and made satisfaction to the injured law. Now both the sinner and the Surety are free.

This is a great joy, a joy for which to make the golden harps ring out a loftier style of music. He who took our debt has now delivered himself from it by dying on the cross. His new life, now that He has risen from the dead, is a life free from legal claim, and it is the token to us that we whom He represented are free also. Listen! "Who shall lay anything to the charge of God's elect? It is God that justifieth. Who is he that condemneth? It is Christ that died, yea rather, that is risen again" (Rom. 8:33, 34). It is a knockdown blow to fear when the apostle says that we cannot be condemned because Christ has died in our stead, but he puts a double force into it when he cries, "Yea rather, that is risen again." If Satan, therefore, shall come to any believer and say, "What about your sin?" tell him Jesus died for it, and your sin is put away. If he come a second time, and say to you, "What about your sin?" answer him, "Jesus lives, and His life is the assurance of our justification; for if our Surety had not paid the debt He would still be under the power of death." Inasmuch as Jesus has discharged all our liabilities, and left not one farthing due to God's justice from one of His people, He lives and is clear, and we live in Him, and are clear also by virtue of our union with Him. Is not this a glorious doctrine, this doctrine of the resurrection, in its bearing upon the justification of the saints? The Lord Jesus gave himself for our sins, but He rose again for our justification.

Bear with me while I notice, next, another bearing of this resurrection of Christ. It *was a guarantee of His people's resurrection.* There is a great truth that never is to be forgotten, namely, that Christ and His people are one just as Adam and all his seed are one. That which Adam did he did as a head for a body, and as our Lord Jesus and all believers are one, so that which Jesus did He did as a head for a body. We were crucified together with Christ, we were buried with Christ, and we are risen together with Him; yea, He hath raised us up together and made us sit together in the heavenly places in Christ Jesus. He says, "Because I live ye shall live also." If Christ be not raised from the dead your faith is vain, and our preaching is vain, and yè are yet in your sins, and those that have fallen asleep in Christ have perished, and you will perish too; but if Christ has been raised from the dead then all his people must be raised also; it is a matter of gospel necessity. There is no logic more imperative than the argument drawn from union with Christ. God has made the saints one with Christ, and if Christ has risen all the saints must rise too. My soul takes firm hold on this and as she strengthens her grasp she loses all fear of death. Now we bear our dear ones to the cemetery and leave them each one in his narrow cell, calmly bidding him farewell and saying:

> So Jesus slept: God's dying Son
> Pass'd through the grave, and blest the bed;
> Rest here, dear saint, till from His throne
> The morning break, and pierce the shade.

It is not merely ours to know that our brethren are living in heaven, but also that their mortal parts are in divine custody, securely kept till the appointed hour when the body shall be reanimated, and the perfect man shall enjoy the adoption of God. We are sure that our dead men shall live; together with Christ's dead body they shall rise. No power can hold in durance the redeemed of the Lord. "Let my people go" shall be a command as much obeyed by death as once by the humbled Pharaoh who could not hold a single Israelite in bonds. The day of deliverance cometh on apace.

> Break from His throne, illustrious morn!
> Attend, O earth, His sovereign word;
> Restore thy trust, a glorious form:
> He must ascend to meet his Lord.

Once more, our Lord's *rising from the dead is a fair picture of the new life which all believers already enjoy.* Beloved, though this body is still subject to bondage like the rest of the visible creation, according to the law stated in Scripture, "the body is dead because of sin," yet "the spirit is life because of righteousness." The regeneration which has taken place in those who believe has changed our spirit, and given to it eternal life, but it has not affected our body further than this, that it has made it to be the temple of the Holy Spirit, and thus it is a holy thing, and cannot be obnoxious to the Lord, or swept away among unholy things; but still the body is subject to pain and weariness, and to the supreme sentence of death. Not so the spirit. There is within us already a part of the resurrection accomplished, since it is written, "and you hath he quickened who were dead in trespasses and sins" (Eph. 2:1). You once were like the ungodly, under the law of sin and death, but you have been brought out of the bondage of corruption into the liberty of life and grace: the Lord having wrought in you gloriously, "according to the working of his mighty power, which he wrought in Christ, when he raised him from the dead, and set him at his own right hand in the heavenly places" (Eph. 1:19, 20).

Now, just as Jesus Christ led, after His resurrection, a life very different from that before His death, so you and I are called upon to live a high and noble spiritual and heavenly life, seeing that we have been raised from the dead to die no more. Let us joy and rejoice in this. Let us behave as those who are alive from the dead, the happy children of the Resurrection. Do not let us be money-grubbers, or hunters after worldly fame. Let us now set our affections on the foul things of this dead and rotten world, but let our hearts fly upward, like young birds that have broken loose of their shells—upward towards our Lord and the heavenly things upon which He would have us set our minds. Living truth, living work, living faith, these are the things for living men: let us cast off the grave-clothes of our former lusts, and wear the garments of light and life. May the Spirit of God help us in further meditating upon these things at home.

Bearings of the Resurrection Upon the Gospel

Now, secondly, let us consider the *bearings of this fact of the resurrection upon the Gospel*; for Paul says, "Jesus Christ was raised from the dead *according to my gospel*." I always like to see what way any kind of statement bears on the gospel. I may not have many more opportunities of preaching, and I make up my mind to this one thing, that I will waste no time upon secondary themes, but when I do preach it shall be the gospel, or something very closely bearing upon it. I will endeavor each time to strike under the fifth rib, and never beat the air. Those who have a taste for the superfluities may take their fill of them, it is for me to keep to the great necessary truths by which men's souls are saved. My work is to preach Christ crucified and the gospel, which gives men salvation through faith. I hear every now and then of men preaching sermons about some bright new nothing or another. Some preachers remind me of the emperor who had a wonderful skill in carving men's heads upon cherry stones. What a multitude of preachers we have who can make wonderfully fine discourses out of a mere passing thought, of no consequence to anyone. But we want the gospel. We have to live and die, and we must have the gospel. Certain of us may be cold in our graves before many weeks are over, and we cannot afford to toy and trifle: we want to see the bearings of all teachings upon our eternal destinies, and upon the gospel which sheds its light over our future.

The resurrection of Christ is vital, because first it tells

us that *the gospel is the gospel of a living Savior.* We have not to send poor penitents to the crucifix, the dead image of a dead man. We say not, "These be the gods, O Israel!" We have not to send you to a little baby Christ nursed by a woman. Nothing of the sort. Behold the Lord that liveth and was dead and is alive forevermore, and hath the keys of hell and of death! Behold in Him a living and accessible Savior who out of the glory still cries with loving accents, "Come unto me, all ye that labor and are heavy laden, and I will give you rest" (Matt. 11:28). "He is able also to save them to the uttermost that come unto God by him, seeing he ever liveth to make intercession for them" (Heb. 7:25). I say we have a living Savior, and is not this a glorious feature of the gospel?

Notice next that we *have a powerful Savior* in connection with the gospel that we preach; for He who had power to raise himself from the dead, has all power now that He is raised. He who in death vanquishes death, can much more conquer by His life. He who being in the grave did, nevertheless, burst all its bonds, can assuredly deliver all His people. He who, coming under the power of the law, did, nevertheless, fulfill the law, and thus set His people free from bondage, must be mighty to save. You need a Savior strong and mighty, yet you do not want one stronger than He of whom it is written that He rose again from the dead. What a blessed gospel we have to preach,— the gospel of a living Christ who hath himself returned from the dead leading captivity captive.

And now notice, that we have *the gospel of complete justification* to preach to you. We do not come and say, "Brethren, Jesus Christ by His death did something by which men may be saved if they have a mind to be, and diligently carry out their good resolves." No, no; we say Jesus Christ took the sin of His people upon himself and bore the consequences of it in His own body on the tree, so that He died; and having died, and so paid the penalty, He lives again; and now all for whom He died, all His people whose sins He bore, are free from the guilt of sin. You ask me, "Who are they?" and I reply, as many as believe on Him. Whosoever believeth in Jesus Christ is as free from the guilt of sin as Christ is. Our Lord Jesus took the sin of His people, and died in the sinner's stead, and now being himself set free, all His people are set free in their Representative. This doctrine is worth preaching. One may well rise from his bed to talk about perfect justification through faith in Christ Jesus. One might as well keep asleep as rise to say that Jesus accomplished little or nothing by His passion and His rising. Some seem to dream that Jesus made some little opening by which we have a slight chance of reaching pardon and eternal life, if we are diligent for many years. This is not our gospel. Jesus has saved His people. He has performed the work entrusted to Him. He has finished transgression, made an end of sin, and brought in everlasting righteousness, and whosoever believeth in Him is not condemned, and never can be.

Once again, the connection of the resurrection and the gospel is this, *it proves the safety of the saints,* for if when Christ rose His people rose also, they rose to a life like that of their Lord, and therefore they can never die. It is written, "Christ being raised from the dead dieth no more; death hath no more dominion over him" (Rom. 6:9), and it is so with the believer: if you have been dead with Christ and are risen with Christ, death has no more dominion over you; you shall never go back to the beggarly elements of sin, you shall never become what you were before your regeneration. You shall never perish, neither shall any pluck you out of Jesus' hand. He has put within you a living and incorruptible seed which liveth and abideth forever. He says himself, "The water that I shall give him shall be in him a well of living water springing up unto everlasting life" (John 4:14). Wherefore hold ye fast to this, and let the resurrection of your Lord be the pledge of your own final perseverance.

Brethren, I cannot stop to show you how this resurrection touches the gospel at ever point, but Paul is always full of it. More than thirty times Paul talks about the resurrection, and occasionally at great length, giving whole chapters to the glorious theme. The more I think of it the more I delight to preach Jesus and the resurrection.

The glad tidings that Christ has risen is as truly the gospel as the doctrine that He came among men and for men presented His blood as a ransom. If angels sang glory to God in the highest when the the Lord was born, I feel impelled to repeat the note now that he is risen from the dead.

Bearing of the Resurrection Upon Ourselves

And so I come to my last head, and to the practical conclusion: *the bearing of this resurrection upon ourselves.* Paul expressly bids us "Remember" it. "Why," says one, "we don't forget it." Are you sure you do not? I find myself far too forgetful of divine truths. We ought not to forget, for this first day of the week is consecrated for sabbatic purposes to constrain us to think of the resurrection. On the seventh day men celebrated a finished creation, on the first day we celebrate a finished redemption. Bear it, then, in mind. Now, if you will remember that Jesus Christ of the seed of David rose from the dead, what will follow?

First, you will find that m*ost of your trials will vanish.* Are you tried by your sins? Jesus Christ rose again from the dead for your justification. Does Satan accuse? Jesus rose to be your advocate and intercessor. Do infirmities hinder? The living Christ will show himself strong on your behalf. You have a living Christ, and in him you have all things. Do you dread death? Jesus, in rising again, has vanquished the last enemy. He will come and meet you when it is your turn to pass through the chill stream, and you shall ford it in sweet company. What is your trouble? I care not what it is, for if you will only think of Jesus as living, full of power, full of love, and full of sympathy, having experienced all your trials, even unto death, you will have such a confidence in His tender care and in His boundless ability that you will follow in His footsteps without a question. Remember Jesus, and that he rose again from the dead, and your confidence will rise as on eagles' wings.

Next, remember Jesus, for then you will see how your present sufferings are as nothing compared with His sufferings, and you will learn to *expect victory over your sufferings even as He obtained victory.* Kindly look at 2 Timothy 2, and you will find the apostle there saying in the third verse, "Thou therefore endure hardness, as a good soldier of Jesus Christ," and further on in the eleventh verse, "It is a faithful saying: for if we be dead in him, we shall also live in him: if we suffer, we shall also reign with him." Now, then, when you are called to suffer, think,— "Jesus suffered, yet Jesus rose again from the dead; he came up out of his baptism of griefs the better and more glorious for it, and so shall I!" Wherefore go you into the furnace at the Lord's bidding, and do not fear that the smell of fire shall pass upon you. Go you even down into the grave, and do not think that the worm shall make an end of you any more than it did of him. Behold in the risen One the type and model of what you are and are to be! Wherefore fear not, for Christ conquered! Stand not trembling, but march boldly on, for Jesus Christ of the seed of David rose from the dead, and you who are of the seed of the promise shall rise again from all your trials and afflictions, and live a glorious life.

We see here, dear brethren, in being told to remember Jesus that *there is hope even in our hopelessness.* When are things most hopeless in a man? Why, when he is dead! Do you know what it is to come down to that, so far as your inward weakness is concerned? I do. At times it seems to be that all my joy is buried like a dead thing, and all my present usefulness and all my hope of being useful in the future are coffined and laid underground like a corpse. In the anguish of my spirit, and the desolation of my heart, I could count it better to die than to live. You say it should not be so. I grant you it should not be so, but so it is. Many things happen within the minds of poor mortals which should not happen; if we had more courage and more faith they would not happen. Ay, but when we go down, down, down, is it not a blessed thing that Jesus Christ of the seed of David died, and was raised from the dead? If I sink right down among the dead men yet will I hold to this blessed hope, that as Jesus rose again from the dead, so also shall my joy, my usefulness, my hope, my spirit rise. "Thou, which hast showed us great and sore troubles, shalt quicken us again, and bring us up from the lowest depths of the earth" (Ps. 71:20). This downcasting and slaying is good for us. We take a deal of killing, and it is by being killed that we live. Many a man will never live till his proud self is slain. O proud Pharisee, if you are to live among those whom God accepts, you will have to come to the slaughterhouse and be cut in pieces as well as killed. "This is dreadful work," saith one, "this dividing of joints and marrow, this spiritual dismemberment and destruction." Assuredly it is painful, and yet it were a grievous loss to be denied it. Alas, how many are so good and excellent, and strong and wise, and clever, and all that, that they cannot agree to be saved by grace through faith. If they could be reduced to less than nothing it would be the finest thing that ever happened to them.

Remember what Solomon said might be done with the fool, and yet it would not answer—he was to be brayed in a mortar among wheat with a pestle,—pretty hard dealing that, and yet his folly would not depart from him. Not by that process alone, but through some such method, the Holy Spirit brings men away from their folly. Under his killing operations this may be their comfort that, if Jesus Christ rose literally from the dead (not from sickness, but from death), and lives again, even so will His people. Did you ever get, where John Bunyan pictures Christian as getting, right under the old dragon's foot? He is very heavy, and presses the very breath out of a fellow when he makes him his footstool. Poor Christian lay there with the dragon's foot on his breast; but he was just able to stretch out his hand and lay hold on his sword, which, by a good providence, lay within his reach. Then he gave Apollyon a deadly thrust, which made him spread his dragon wings and fly away. The poor crushed and broken pilgrim, as he gave the stab to his foe, cried, "Rejoice not over me, O mine enemy; though I fall, yet shall I rise again." Brother, do you the same. You that are near despair, let this be the strength that nerves your arm and steels your heart. "Jesus Christ of the seed of David was raised from the dead according to Paul's gospel" (2 Tim. 2:8).

Lastly, this proves the *futility of all opposition to Christ*. The learned are going to destroy the Christian religion. Already, according to their boastings, it has pretty nearly come to an end. The pulpit is effete, it cannot command public attention. We stand up and preach to empty benches! As you see—*or do not see*. Nothing remains for us but to die decently, so they insinuate. And what then? When our Lord was dead, when the clay-cold corpse lay, watched by the Roman soldiery, and with a seal upon the enclosing stone, was not the cause in mortal jeopardy? But how fared it? Did it die out? Every disciple that Jesus had made forsook Him, and fled, was not Christianity then destroyed? Nay, that very day our Lord won a victory which shook the gates of hell, and caused the universe to stand astonished. Matters are not worse with Him at this hour! His affairs are not in a sadder condition today than then. Nay, see Him today and judge. On His head are many crowns, and at His feet the hosts of angels bow! Jesus is the master of legions today, while the Caesars have passed away! Here are His people—needy, obscure, despised, I grant you, still, but assuredly somewhat more numerous than they were when they laid Him in the tomb. His cause is not to be crushed, it is forever rising.

Year after year, century after century, bands of true and honest hearts are marching up to the assault of the citadel of Satan. The prince of this world has a stronghold here on earth, and we are to capture it; but as yet we see small progress, for rank after rank the warriors of the Lord have marched to the breach and disappeared beneath the terrible fire of death. All who have gone before seem to have been utterly cut off and destroyed, and still the enemy holds his ramparts against us. Has nothing been done, think you? Has death taken away those martyrs, and confessors, and preachers, and laborious saints, and has nothing been achieved? Truly if Christ were dead I would admit our defeat, for they that are fallen asleep in Him would have perished: but as Christ liveth so the cause liveth, and they that have fallen are not dead: they have vanished from our sight for a little, but if the curtain could be withdrawn every one of them would be seen to stand in his lot unharmed, crowned, victorious! "Who are these arrayed in white robes, and whence came they?" (Rev. 7:13). These are they that were defeated! Whence, then, their crowns? These are they that were dishonored! Whence then their white robes? These are they who clung to a cause which is overthrown. Whence then their long life of victors, for there is not a vanquished man among them all?

Let the truth be spoken. Defeat is not the word for the cause of Jesus, the Prince of the house of David. We have always been victorious, brethren; we are victorious now. Follow your Master on your white horses, and be not afraid! I see Him in the front with His blood-stained vesture around Him, fresh from the wine-press where He has trodden down His foes. You have not to present atoning blood, but only to conquer after your Lord. Put on your white raiment and follow Him on your white horses, conquering and to conquer. He is nearer than we think, and the end of all things may be before the next jibe shall have come forth from the mouth of the last new skeptic. Have confidence in the risen One, and live in the power of His resurrection.

The Unrecognized Victory

J. Stuart Holden (1874-1934), Vicar of St. Paul's Church, Portman Square, London, was an Anglican preacher of great ability. Possessing an engaging personality and persuasive manner, Holden was known on both sides of the Atlantic for his convention ministries. Holden was leader of the Keswick movement for almost 30 years and guided it ably. Skilled as a diagnostician of the deeper spiritual life, he helped guide many in discerning the difference between spurious and genuine faith.

This message on God's mercy is from *Life's Flood-tide* by J. Stuart Holden, published by Roxburghe House, London, 1913.

J. Stuart Holden

11

THE UNRECOGNIZED VICTORY

They have taken away my Lord, and I know not where they have laid Him (John 20:13).

THE RESURRECTION IS the most essentially and entirely divine of all Christ's works. It stands out forever as at once the mightiest miracle and deepest mystery connected with His redeeming work. The significance of its power is beyond all human conception or measure. For, if it be not true, the whole claim and promise of grace is confounded. But if it be true that Jesus burst the bands of death and revealed Himself as Death's conqueror, then all the claim He ever put forth is substantiated, and all the promise He ever made is confirmed. When we view its simple and stupendous action in the Gospel records, we are face to face with the supreme revelation and measure of the divine power. Victory over sin and death, and a living hope for the sons of men, are its clarion notes of triumph. God in all His might is seen without any veiling medium. And we are at the same time uplifted in His greatness and humbled in our own littleness.

Yet its story of triumphant power is wonderfully interwoven with some of the most tender and human stories which the whole history of God's ways with men contains. For example, what could be more beautiful than the account of that sabbath evening walk to Emmaus? And how often, indeed, has it been repeated in actual fact in this our own day, as disciples of Christ have walked together after worship on sabbath evenings? Many a time has the Risen Lord walked with them just as of old, intertwining His friendship with theirs, and affording them indubitable proofs that He is alive from the dead! Or what more simple than the record of His appearance to the eleven in the upper room, hallowed by such precious memory! Or what more heartening than His reassuring talk with the sorely puzzled Thomas? Or what could bring His tenderness nearer to the hearts of His people than His persuasive questioning of the downcast Peter, or His kindly care for the hungry fishermen in the preparation with His own hands of breakfast for them?

All these simple and beautifully human stories are given to us as parts of the first Easter story, as though to emphasize the fact that the precious jewel of truth is to be set in the common and ordinary circumstances which go to make up the life of us all, that its beauties may be realized and reflected.

Mary Magdalene

But of all these stories (whose simplicity and naturalness, be it said, are a large part of their credibility), perhaps the most moving and human of all is that of Mary Magdalene. During Christ's lifetime she had loved Him much, being much forgiven. He had accepted the ministry of affection at her hands, and had enriched her, as is always His way, by what He had taken from her. Now He is dead. And in the awful numbness of her sorrow she has, for the time, at any rate, forgotten all His promises of resurrection; so she hastens to the tomb to lavish upon His dead body the love which His recent sufferings have fanned into a quenchless flame.

But, alas! for her intentions—the tomb is empty. Hardly knowing what she is doing, she runs to the disciples and announces that Christ's body has been taken away, that calamity has succeeded calamity, that any lingering hope of seeing Him again as of old is gone! Forgetful, like her, of His foretold resurrection, two of them—Peter and John—run to the tomb; and having satisfied themselves that what she says is true, and accepting their first impressions as trustworthy, they go away again to their own home.

But Mary cannot leave the spot made so sacred by His association. She remains there to weep and to think of Him who has forever made the old life impossible to her, even though she is never to see His face again. Through her tears, as through a mist, she sees two strange figures in white, but knows them not to be the heralds of the King who is even at that moment coming to set up His Kingdom within her in a fuller and truer sense than ever before. They, for their part, marvel at seeing her tears at such a time; for surely the night of weeping is gone and unspeakable joy has come with this morning. But to their question she can but respond with the hopelessness of despair—"They have taken away my Lord!" Then, turning round, for the first time she sees Christ whom her soul loveth in the beauty of His risen life! Then when He has made Himself known to her and has convinced her that He is truly alive, heaven opens indeed, and she sees "the angels of God ascending and descending upon the Son of Man."

The Point of the Story

Now the point of this beautiful story of the first Easter morning is in the possibility of one who truly loves Christ so entirely misconceiving the great event. She was in the presence of the greatest of all victories without recognizing it. The signs she saw were not of defeat but of triumph. But she misread them all. She had not lost Christ, as she feared, but had really found Him more fully than she had ever before known Him. She was not at the end but rather at the beginning of all things. It was a day for praise and great joy, not for weeping. She thought that the service she had come to render to Him in the tomb was now forever impossible. But in reality there was opened to her that day a life of service greater and more far-reaching than all her wildest love-dreams. Yes! Hers was the pathetic tragedy, so common in this our own day, of an unrecognized victory.

It is not too much to say that in all the churches, and outside of them too, there are those who seem unable to grasp the essential fact that the Savior of the world is no longer the dead Christ of a bygone age, the central figure of a purely local event, but the Risen Lord, unconfined in His work by time or place, and universal in His scope and range of power. We are always in danger of misconceiving God's workings, as though they were the doings of others;

of seeing calamity in every change; of being blind to all but outward things; of imagining that a temporary darkness (necessitated by our own weakness of eyes) is a total eclipse. Now it is not faith, but faithlessness, which looks out upon the world today, and says in tones of concern, "They have taken away my Lord." As though He *could* be taken away! Truly the greatest need, both in individual and corporate Christian life, is to know the reality of the resurrection, and to recognize that He who is "alive forevermore" is fulfilling Himself in a thousand ways in the hearts of men. For Christ is bigger than our conceptions, and cannot be confined in our creeds. Hence, panic may well give way to praise, and concern to courage. For not only is He the Christ of the bounded past but of the boundless present also. We may always see the place where the Lord lay, and it is right we should often thankfully visit it. But we shall make an eternal mistake if we imagine He is always to be found there, and there only. For such thought attests our failure to recognize the victory, and hence to share it.

What Does It Mean?

"They have taken away my Lord." This is frequently the language of those who think that Christ has been taken away by the growing apprehension of His Truth on the part of His people. Men do not lay stress today on doctrines which in former years were regarded as of vital importance. Language and phraseology have changed, and with them many of the formulae of faith so dear to our fathers have become almost obsolete. The message of the Evangel is delivered with new-placed emphasis. Time-worn methods of expression are frankly abandoned in favor of others which seem more fully to reflect the mind of Christ Himself, and are certainly more easily understood and readily responded to by the men of the present. Under the influence of modern thought, creeds are questioned, indeed, are often frankly abandoned, while character, and not orthodoxy, is insisted upon as the essential expression of true faith. Dogma is apt to be suspected, while the devotional life is urged. The old and terrifying doctrines of the sternness of God are, to an extent, discounted, or at any rate cast into shadow, by the discovery or rediscovery of His prevailing sympathy. The call to Christ in order to save oneself is replaced by the call to Christ in order to be fitted to save others. The divine Fatherhood is being expressed in terms of the human brotherhood. And the Gospel of today insists that Christ came not to save men's souls with a view to their entering heaven in the future, but to save men's lives with a view to their enriching earth in the present.

Now all this appears very sad and calamitous to many truly good people, who imagine the interests of the Kingdom to be bound up with certain well-defined articles of belief, and who are unable to appreciate the difference between Truth and human appreciation of it—between the divine fact and the human form in which it is expressed. They think that the divine feet must always tread the pathway of their theology in His drawing near to men. In fact, their mistake is in believing that Christ has been taken away by the very development of men's conscious apprehension of Him, whereas in reality He has been brought infinitely nearer. For as on that earliest Easter day when Mary first made this now so common mistake, Christ is not in the grave but in the garden. He is not in the place of death, but in the place of life and growth and beauty. As in nature life is always expressing itself in new forms, so the living Christ in the living world is always expressing Himself in ways of forceful and fruitful appeal to every age.

The gospel of the Risen Lord rightly apprehended will save us from all unbelieving alarm, and will correct all anxious misreading of the miracle and victory of the Life indeed. Mary went to the tomb expecting to find things there just as she had preconceived them. The revelation of the Risen Christ, however, falsified all her thoughts and magnified all her unspoken hopes. And still He lives to rebuke our faithlessness, and to end all our unworthy notions of His power, as the rising sun pales the morning star, its forerunner.

"They have taken away my Lord." This, too, is frequently

the judgment of many, who conclude that their hard and severe experiences of life have robbed them of the Christ of grace and love. Disappointment, disaster, and discouragement all seem to create for them an empty tomb. They have known Christ in His early gifts of peace and pardon, have sat at His feet to learn the elementary lessons of His Kingdom, have followed Him in the pathways of service, and have experienced something of His power both within and through them. But now all is changed. The light of the morning has faded into cold gloom. Unexpected experiences have overtaken them; and the Christ whose love served them well in other days seems to be no longer available—at any rate effectively. Now, as a matter of fact, such ones, like Mary Magdalene, are in the presence of a miracle, and do not know it! For the Risen Lord, who long ago began the work of transformation in them, is really working by means of these very experiences to bring them into fuller and more intimate knowledge of Himself. They are missing Him by misinterpreting His ways.

A Poignant Illustration

George Macdonald puts into the mouth of one of his characters who is suffering the smart of sorrow and the discipline of suffering the petulant cry:

"I wish I'd never been made!"

To which her friend replies: "My dear, you're not made yet. You're only being made, and are finding fault with the Maker's process!"

Now this is just what many are doing. They regard as perversity what is really a loving providence. They look upon a divinely meant beatitude as a blunder. Their backs are turned to the Risen Christ, while their eyes are fixed upon the empty tomb. In their quest they are missing the conquest. They are bewailing their loss when they might be beholding their Lord, and gaining in His fellowship a satisfactory explanation of all the perplexing things which have helped to make possible this knowledge of Him. For since He is alive, such things as He orders can never take Him away. Any idea to the contrary may always be regarded as a false conclusion, and resisted as disloyal unbelief.

When the history of the scientific discovery and attainment of the past decade comes to be written, one of the most striking chronicles will be that of the transformation of the by-products of coal-tar into perfumes, dyes, and drugs. Modern chemistry has taken the black, unlovely substance and, as with a magic touch, has transmuted it into fragrance and beauty and usefulness. And this is but one of nature's many parables of this resurrection lesson! Let us be careful lest life becomes permanently improverished by the tragedy of the unrecognized victory.

"They have taken away my Lord." In what a different sense are these words sometimes used by those who are conscious that willful sin has robbed them of all conscious enjoyment of Christ's presence. Self-indulgence, absorption in some unsurrendered and unregulated pursuit of business or pleasure or rebellious self-will, have brought a desolating sense of lost purity, forfeited peace, and inner disorder. Truly, "they have taken away my Lord." For Barabbas, who is the only alternative to Christ in every moral crisis in which choice is imperative, is always a robber! And no mere words can bring back the sense of Christ's friendship nor the heart-influence of His nearness. The defiled conscience must be cleansed. The debilitated will must be strengthened into a new consecration. And only Christ Himself can effect this miracle. But He can! This is the gospel of the resurrection; that He who of old cleansed the leper, strengthened the paralyzed, and raised the dead, is alive to do these same things for men today. How many there are who look wistfully back to boyhood's days of faith and purity when Christ seemed near and dear to them, and heaven lay round about them. But much water has flowed under the bridge since those golden days, and between that time and this there stands a record of countless accusing sins; so that the heart, awakened to a disgust of its own weak yieldings, says in sorrow and despair, "They have taken away my Lord."

If you are in such a case do not be tempted to think

that the past is invincibly and eternally your master. Were it not for the Resurrection it certainly would be. But "now is Christ risen!" Hence there is a living hope of deliverance and full salvation for every bound and burdened one. He can take away the very things which appear to have taken Him away from you. And that He does so is attested by the experience of all who have ever drawn near to Him in penitence and prayer.

A Wonderful Revelation

Oh! what a wonderful revelation of Himself did Mary gain, on the very heels of her greatest mistake! For He whom she had imagined was forever lost to her, gave proof of His intimate and undying care in the use of the old name by which He addressed her—"Mary." The Risen Lord gently reminds her of all the past, now so inextricably bound up with Himself, as though to encourage her to still greater trust in the One who knows all about her, and whose love surpasses His knowledge. Then, as in an impulsive way she stretches out her hands to clasp His, He at once lifts their intimacy on to that higher plane of spiritual fellowship, where she shall henceforth be independent of all external media in the heart-communion with Him, which is to qualify for all future life and service. And in His gentle rebuke, and to assure her again of the miracle of which she is the first witness, He proclaims a new and amazing blood-brotherhood—"My Father and your Father!" Nor is it to be wondered at that such a stimulus to the heart should quicken the footsteps; and that she who had at first failed to recognize the victory should now run to those who had heard her cry, "They have taken away my Lord," with the triumphant tidings "that she had seen the Lord, and that He had spoken these things unto her!"

Thus her awakening to the mightiest fact of all about the Son of God is just a picture of that correction of impulsive faithlessness, and expansion of imperfect faith which ever follows the revelation of the Living Lord to His people. As with her testimony, so too with theirs in this and every age. "They have taken away my Lord,"

gives place to the grand Evangel of the Resurrection, "He
hath given us eternal life, and this life is in His Son!" Nor
will those who know it for themselves be content until
they have sounded it forth throughout all His World. For
the world's greatest need is to recognize the victory of the
One who liveth and was dead, and behold is alive
forevermore!

He Rises Again

William E. Sangster (1900-1960) was the "John Wesley" of his generation as he devoted his life to evangelism and the promotion of practical sanctification. He pastored in England and Wales, and his preaching ability attracted the attention of the Methodist leaders. He ministered during World War II at Westminster Central Hall, London, where he pastored the church, managed an air-raid shelter in the basement, and studied for his Ph.D. at the London University! He served as president of the Methodist Conference (1950) and director of the denomination's home missions and evangelism ministry. He published several books on preaching, sanctification, and evangelism, as well as volumes of sermons.

This message comes from *Westminster Sermons*, volume two, published in 1961 by The Epworth Press, London.

William E. Sangster

12

HE RISES AGAIN

The stone was rolled away (Mark 16:4).

IT IS A PAINFULLY small ministry that can be exercised upon the body of our dead—yet love always insists on offering it. The last sad offices are performed with a studious care which shows how keenly our broken hearts bewail the finality of service; a clod is precious that has housed a much-loved soul.

Even the deserted and crucified Son of God had dear ones who were anxious to offer this last expression of devotion to Him. There were women who set out early for the place of His burial. Their eagerness is shown in the manner of their coming. Mark and Luke tell us that they were hastening to the sepulcher "very early in the morning." Matthew says "as it began to dawn." John says "when it was yet dark"—these women came bearing the spices in their hands; blessedly zealous over the useless; with the desperation of love, which *will* find service, they came to make that wearied body restful for the long night of death.

Nor is their haste shown only by the hour of their coming. It is revealed, also, in the very composition of the party. There was no man in it!—and the sepulcher was sealed with a stone and the stone was "very great." Perhaps they hardly thought of this in their hasty departure, but it came to them on the way and they murmured to one another, "Who shall roll us away the stone from the door of the tomb?" Then they arrive! . . . *and the stone is rolled away!* . . . *and the sepulcher is empty* . . . and a white-robed youth addresses them: "Be not amazed: ye seek Jesus, the Nazarene which hath been crucified. He is risen: He is not here: Behold the place where they laid Him" (Mark

16:5,6). And the women fled from the tomb in astonishment, trembling, speechless and afraid.

That was the most glorious dawn in human history! There was a radiance in the golden light of that morning the world had never known before.

What Stone Was Rolled Away?

Let us explore the heart of this sublime event with three questions—questions which may seem a little naive when you first hear them. Here is the first. *What stone was rolled away?*

Make no effort to hide the fact. Death is the great enigma of life. Humanly speaking, it is an insoluble mystery; it is the one secret of the universe which is kept; the silence which is never broken. Death is one of the rare things which can be predicted of all men; the common end to a path of glory or a road of shame. To the weary and despairing it may come as a friend; the cynical and disillusioned may meet it with indifference; to the healthy and happy it may appear as a foe, but as friend, or foe, or cold companion, it comes to all. All our plans for the future are made subject to its approval. There is no earthly tie too sacred for death to loosen. It reduces the exalted and the lowly to the common denominator of dust.

Moreover, the mystery is as old as mankind. From the dimmest beginnings of history, we find men pondering the problem of the beyond. In the upward movement of mankind we find them nursing their hopes on a variety of dreams, and passing in turn from belief in a dim spirit life to the shadowy existence called Sheol, and finally to the vision of a life fuller and grander than this. But it was still a mystery. These dreams were . . . *dreams*; interesting speculations, but nothing more. Death was still "the undiscovered country from whose bourn no traveler returns." This was the great stone that blocked the path of human aspiration. What certitude was there of the continuity of life? What modest man could find in himself anything worthy to endure for all eternity? Of what abiding worth was love even—our highest—if it ended in the passionless calm of death?

Then came the first Easter day and—*the stone was rolled away!* That stone! Mark says it was "exceeding heavy." And now it is rolled away, for one Traveler returned. Death is an abysmal cavern no more, but a tunnel with a golden light at the farther end. It is no more a blind alley, but a thoroughfare; no more a cul-de-sac, but a highway. The mystery is a mystery no more. "'Tis Death is dead, not He." "And," says Paul, "if the spirit of Him that raised up Jesus from the dead dwell in you, He that raised up Jesus from the dead shall quicken also your mortal bodies by His spirit that dwelleth in you" (Rom. 8:11).

The stone is rolled away and justifies the blessed contradictoriness of the phrase in the burial service, "the sure and certain hope [a *certain hope?*] of everlasting life."

Why Was the Stone Rolled Away?

Here is the second question. *Why was the stone rolled away?*

Surely it was not rolled away that the Risen Lord might come out? Of whatever nature was His resurrection body, the Lord Jesus was independent of doors and indifferent to walls. John explicitly tells us: "Jesus cometh, the doors being shut, and stood in the midst and said, Peace be unto you." And yet the stone was rolled away! I think I know why. It was not rolled away that He might come out, but that they might go in. It was no part of the *fact*; it was a part merely of the *demonstration*. It was not the means of His exit, but the means of their entrance. This it is that makes the resurrection more than a piece of history; it makes it also a pledge. This lifts it above the level of mere news and makes it a promise, for God rolled away the stone, not that His Son might rise, but that we might know He had risen; that we might steal into the empty tomb and see only "the place where they laid Him."

Do I make the distinction clear? Let me illustrate! Let us suppose that a child was entrusted to my care and it fell to my lot one night to put him to bed. I would take him, I suppose, to his room and hear his prayers and tuck him in . . . with all the good intention and all the awkwardness of a mere man. And then, as I am about to leave the room and take the light with me, suppose the little fellow falteringly confesses a childish fear to me; tells me that he lives in dread of the other side of that dark and heavy curtain in the corner; that he is foolishly afraid that there is something evil on the farther side, and in the darkness he can almost see some sinister shape emerge to do him harm. . . .

Well! I could leave the room with one peremptory word in my adult awareness that his fear is baseless . . . but I am far too concerned about his peace of mind for that. So I go to the shadowed corner of the room and fling the curtain aside, and flood the dark recess with light and show the groundlessness of his fears; smile the assurance of my love upon him and say: "See? There is *nothing* to fear." My removal of the curtain is no part of the removal of evil, but it is part of the removal of his dread. I have come down to his level that he may find peace, and I am rewarded by seeing him fall calmly asleep.

So God rolled away the stone! It was not necessary for the resurrection of the Lord, but it was necessary for its wider publication. It wasn't necessary that Christ might rise, but it was an impressive and unforgettable part of the proclamation of that fact.

What Did That Rolled-Away Stone Reveal?

Here is the third question. *What did that rolled-away stone reveal?*

Let us follow the women into the tomb. It is a great hole, you see, hewn in a rock. What? Do you shrink a little because it is a tomb? Did you say it makes you feel eerie?

Not here! Not in the *Savior's* tomb! It's empty! There's nothing to be seen: only *the place where they laid Him.*

What went you out to see?

Nothing!

Nothing? Were you satisfied?

It was the most glorious moment of my life.

Amongst the several accounts we have of this tomb let us follow most closely the account given in the fourth Gospel. You cannot doubt, I think, that behind this record there is the clear testimony of an eyewitness. Peter and John run together to the tomb. John outruns Peter yet hesitates to go in. Peter pants up behind, but doesn't hesitate for a moment. In he goes and John follows him. When they are standing together in the sepulcher they see the linen clothes lying and "the napkin that was about his head not lying with the linen clothes but wrapped together in a place by itself."

Some scholars have sensed a strange overtone in the Greek word used to describe the head-cloth. I will be frank and say that I do not get the flavor from the Greek myself, but I am glad to share with you what others savor—or think they savor—even when I don't quite get it myself. Some scholars say that the word used about the head-cloth suggests that it still had an annular shape. It was lying apart from the other clothes and still had the outline of His head

> —the sacred head once wounded
> —With grief and pain weighed down—

still had the form of that "dear disfigured face," the visage more marred than any man's.

Do you get the picture? This is the account of an eyewitness. Does it almost make you feel that you are an eyewitness yourself? Can you see it happen? This was no laborious unwinding! This was a glorious uprising!!

> And all alone alone alone,
> He rose again behind the stone.

How calm and private that blessed sepulcher must have been after all the dreadful and shameful publicity of the Crucifixion. How quiet and still! How blessedly secluded. Jesus loved solitude and He had no solitude between Gethsemane and the sepulcher. Working out the time is difficult, but it seems that eight hours after His arrest He was on the Cross. Eight awful hours! In the brief space of six hours He was examined five times by four different tribunals. In all the haste of their fiendish cruelty they rushed Him from Annas—to Caiaphas—to Pilate—to Herod and back to Pilate again—and then to the Cross. Oh! having driven in the nails and done their devilest, why couldn't they let Him die in quietness and in the company of His dear ones? But no! The cup must be drunk to the dregs and the ghastly publicity of it was part of the bitterness of the Cross.

So as He hangs there—the noise, the dust, the pain, the thirst—and perhaps the incessant noise was not the least of His pangs, the crowds, the jeers, the curses, the sobbing women—and He hangs stark naked between earth and heaven.

O for quietness; for solitude; only to be alone. Through His swimming eyes He sees His mother's face. It brings Nazareth back to Him. Childhood and the fields of Galilee. And John is there. Dear John! "Woman, behold thy son. Son, behold thy mother" (John 19:26,27). And still the noise . . . raucous laughter and bitter sobbing . . . until the blessed numbness steals over His outworn frame . . . and then . . .

"It is finished! Father, into Thy hands I commend my spirit" (John 19:30; Luke 23:46).

And then the sepulcher. Do you still think of a tomb as being cold and eerie? No! No! It is quiet, and calm, and our crucified God rests for hours and hours on a cool bed of rock.

And then (to quote Alice Meynell again):

All alone alone alone,
He rose again behind the stone.

SCRIPTURE TEXT INDEX